30 DAYS TO TAMING WORRY *AND* ANXIETY

Deborah Smith Pegues

HARVEST HOUSE PUBLISHERS
EUGENE, OREGON

Cover by Koechel Peterson & Associates, Minneapolis, Minnesota

Cover Images © Bychykhin Olexandr, wavebreakmedia, BrAt82, Blend Images / Shutterstock

30 DAYS TO TAMING WORRY AND ANXIETY
Copyright © 2007 Deborah Smith Pegues
Published by Harvest House Publishers
Eugene, Oregon 97402
www.harvesthousepublishers.com

ISBN 978-0-7369-6857-7 (pbk.)
ISBN 978-0-7369-6858-4 (eBook)

The Library of Congress has cataloged the earlier edition as follows:
    Pegues, Deborah Smith, 1950-
    30 days to taming your stress / Deborah Smith Pegues.
        p. cm.
    ISBN 978-0-7369-1835-0 (pbk.)
    1. Stress (Psychology—Religious aspects--Christianity. 2. Christian life.
    3. Stress (Psychology—Prevention—Problems, exercises, etc. 4. Stress
    management—Religious aspects—Christianity. I. Title. II. Title: Thirty
    days to taming your stress.
    BV4509.5.P45 2007
    155.9'042—dc22

                                                          2006026725

Printed in the United States of America

    20 21 22 23 24 25 / BP-CD / 10 9 8 7 6 5

*This book is dedicated to the Holy Spirit,
my constant companion and stress reliever.*

Acknowledgments

I am eternally grateful to God for allowing me to be exposed to the following powerful and pure-hearted leaders who model His peace: Bishop Charles Blake, Pastor Edward A. Smith, Bishop E.C. Reems-Dickerson, Dr. Barbara McCoo Lewis, Dr. Elvin Ezekiel, and Bunny Wilson.

J.P., Shannon, and Lainie Sloane, Pamela Johnson, and Sherrone Burke are the best critique-friends one could have. I am also grateful for a host of contributors and intercessors, which include: Marion Meares, Billie Rodgers, Raynae Hernandez, Althea Sims, James Kirkland, Carol Pegues, Creola Waters, Janet Sweet Thomas, Sandra Arceneaux, Sylvia Gardner, Angela Knight, Belinda Wallace, the Kelley family, and many others. My mother, Doris; my father, Rube; and my six brothers: Bobby, Rube Jr., Dale, Reginald, Gene, and Vernon; and their children are my biggest cheerleaders, along with numerous other family members and well-wishers.

I could never find words to express my deep appreciation for the wonderful crew at Harvest House Publishers. They are truly a writer's dream team. My editor, Kim Moore, is phenomenal and extends her assistance beyond editing.

Last, but not least, I am most grateful to my husband, Darnell Pegues, for his patience, steadfast love, and support.

Contents

Prologue

"Your brother is on the line!" yelled my administrative assistant through the half-closed door to my office. It was the second Tuesday of the month, the day of the monthly board of director's meeting at the church where I served as the chief financial officer. The meeting would start in a few hours. I had already instructed her to put through only the most urgent calls on board meeting days as we scrambled to prepare the various financial reports I would present at the meeting. However, the call from my brother was always deemed important because it most likely concerned my mother. I was her conservator—and her only daughter. My heart always skipped a beat when any one of my six brothers called because my mother had suffered a stroke two years earlier and was still struggling to get back to normal physically as well as emotionally.

I grabbed the receiver and put it to my ear a little too quickly. The intense pain in my jaw from the pressure of the phone reminded me that today I was supposed to find a doctor to give me a second opinion on my neurologist's diagnosis of trigeminal neuralgia—a very painful inflamed facial nerve condition. At times the condition had rendered me speechless. Though it really was important to get another opinion, today I could only focus on urgent matters. I'd have to do it tomorrow.

I longed for a nap. I had only slept about four hours the night before because I had stayed up cooking and writing. Though my husband did not expect it, I tried to make sure he had a cooked meal available on nights when I had to work late. I liked the idea of being a domesticated professional woman. It felt right based upon my traditional upbringing. Besides, it took away my guilt for working such outrageous hours. Of course, the time I spent writing was necessary because I had been fortunate enough to land a contract with one of the top Christian publishing houses in the United States. No way was I going to miss my manuscript submission deadline—which was only two weeks away. I was surely going to have to pull some all-nighters to finish on time.

Board meeting days were always guaranteed to be a 12-hour stint since the workday began at 8:30 AM and the meeting did not start until 6:30 PM. As a coping mechanism for my to-do overload, I decided to block out the thought of my upcoming speaking engagement on Saturday morning. I would work on the presentation on Thursday evening—or even Friday, if I could convince my husband to postpone our weekly Friday date night until Sunday after church. I was reluctant to ask him because I wanted to appear to be handling everything with no problems. I couldn't cancel the speaking engagement because the date was too close. Absent an emergency, I never cancel. Besides, speaking is critical for an author's exposure.

Back to my brother. He was calling to tell me that my mother had run out of her most critical medication. The person who was being paid to cover this function had dropped the ball again. I would need to call in the prescription right away so that Gene could pick it up from the pharmacy. As we bemoaned the continued frustration of dealing with my mother's care, I took a quick glance at the financial statement that had just been shoved under my nose to review for the board meeting. There were several glaring errors that threatened to send me over the edge. I wanted to smack the person who had prepared the statement, but I was so hungry I wouldn't have had the energy to engage in this fleeting fantasy anyway. There would be no time for lunch or any type of break today—which meant that I wouldn't be very discriminating in my food selection when things simmered down later. This schedule was wreaking havoc on my body. I was paying the price for working late instead of working out. I closed my eyes and thought, *Oh, for the rapture!* Of course, I did not really mean it. Thinking about being snatched away to be with the Lord for all eternity was just a temporary mental escape from life's demands. *Okay,* I said to myself as I took a long, deep breath, *things could be worse.*

I have a lot to be grateful for, but at that moment, gratitude was not among my chief thoughts. The urgent matters at hand had already grabbed first place in my mind.

On the surface, my life looks idyllic: great husband, great job, great boss, great salary, great family support, great house, great publishing firm—the works. Along with all that, however, came the responsibility for keeping these areas great—and that spelled more demands on my time. Further, as in every person's life, I had some not-so-positive pressures that also tried to threaten my peace. Things such as mediating family conflicts, unexpected car and boat repairs, employee misunderstandings—you know the drill. Of course, as Superwoman, I kept ignoring the nagging pains that were becoming more frequent each day.

While your life events may not parallel mine, I can assure you that if you are reading this book, your own set of daily circumstances are probably producing the same results—stress. Everybody talks about doing something about it eventually, but few people seem to deal with the problem directly and bring it under control.

You have probably heard that the only things in life that are certain are death and taxes. Well, stress can easily be added as a third certainty. It is unavoidable. It was Job who declared, "Man born of woman is of few days and full of trouble" (Job 14:1 NIV). He was right. No one's life is free of stress-producing situations and their physical and emotional impact on our bodies. According to the American Institute for Stress, stress is responsible for 75 to 90 percent of doctor visits in America. Notwithstanding, I believe there is hope. "There is a special rest still waiting for the people of God" (Hebrews 4:8).

Let me warn you that this book is not about how to manage your life to the point of *eliminating* stress, but rather how to respond to it and to minimize the degree to which you experience it. I want you to lock arms with me while we pursue a scripturally based, practical approach to dealing with this problem that impacts people at every level of society. I am not a psychologist, but I am inspired through the divine Word of God. I promise you I will avoid pie-in-the-sky recommendations that only work in theory. What I know for sure is that God wants His children to walk in peace.

Peace is a fruit of the Holy Spirit. If you are not experiencing it, then it is time to confront your stressors—even those you may have worn as a badge of honor—and to get on the road of peace and emotional rest God has ordained for you.

Day 1

Identify Your Stressors

*Please listen and answer me, for I am
overwhelmed by my troubles.*

Psalm 55:2

I have done countless analyses during my career as a financial executive; however, until a couple of years ago, I had never done a stressor analysis in which I listed the situations or people that were bringing pressure to bear upon me and evaluated the extent to which that pressure was impacting me. Stress is our biological response to the pressures of life. The pressures do not necessarily have to be negative to have a negative impact on our bodies, nor must they be the things that are the obvious. I had assumed that things that kept me the busiest would be the primary stressors, but that did not prove to be true. Here are the results of my analysis:

- Mother's housing and health care issues
- My eternal weight loss battle
- Inability to find qualified employees

- Balancing the increasing demands of my dual careers
- My husband's tentativeness about his career objectives

As I pondered my stressors, I objectively categorized them into those I could impact and those outside of my circle of influence. In addition to the major stressors, I also had minor stressors not caused by external situations, but rather by my traditional thinking and entrenched attitudes. While my mother's situation caused me the most concern, I knew that due to certain home ownership issues and her insistence on living in her familiar but problem-ridden environment, I could do very little to make an impact. Therefore, I had to develop an effective coping strategy. I have learned to segment and delay my mental preoccupation with certain situations when other stressors demand my attention. I call it "managing my sanity." God has given me the grace to do it.

My dual career was beginning to require most of my attention. I had felt for the past two years that my season was up as the chief financial officer of the church, but I just couldn't bring myself to tell my boss, even though my husband and others who were sensitive to the voice of God were pressing me to do so. I loved the Bishop. He was the most endearing boss I had ever had. My experience with him was nothing like the horror stories I had heard from my counterparts in other ministries. He rarely called me at home, and if he did, he was very apologetic about it and genuinely needed something that could not wait. I worked crazy hours because I felt that he and the church deserved the same level of effort I had given to companies I had worked for in the corporate world. Notwithstanding, the work never seemed to be done. The job had taken its toll on my health. It was time to take care of myself and time to obey God. Over a two-year period, I had no fewer than ten different highly respected Christian leaders strongly encourage me to go into full-time ministry. I did not want God to have to drag me kicking and screaming to my destiny, so I finally mustered enough courage to tender my resignation. It took five Kleenex tissues for me to tell the Bishop. I cried for the entire month leading up to the final date. I had worked many, many 16-hour or more days. I had even postponed a couple of needed surgeries because I could never find an extended period to be away from the office. I had not realized I was so emotionally invested in the place until I faced the reality that I would no longer be there.

We had built this awesome $66 million cathedral, and I had signed the check for every single item in it. It was featured in several popular magazines. Further, my husband and I had sacrificed and made a significant financial investment in the project. I felt a serious sense of ownership. I knew God was saying, "Okay, mission accomplished." However, I just wanted to settle down and enjoy the fruit of my labor. Plus, I had finally become comfortable with my expertise of every aspect of our operation. It did not seem right to let it all go to waste.

Many times the path to God's perfect will for our lives requires us to make various transitions. For example, to get to San Diego, California, where I often speak, I have to travel on Interstate 10 for a few miles, transition to the 110 Freeway for several more miles, and finally transition to the 405 Freeway for more than 100 miles before I reach San Diego. Obviously, I would never get there if I remained on I-10. Transitions are sometimes mandatory if we want to achieve our destination.

So it is with our ordained destiny. We are created with free will, which is not to say that God does not have a special plan for our lives, yet it is *we* who act outside God's will, therefore missing the blessings He has for us. Many times God is saying, "Time to transition to the next path." But we respond, "I'm very familiar with this route. Can't I just stay here and still reach my destiny?" Then we have the audacity to become frustrated or blame God when our goals seem to elude us.

I had to get real about my stressors, and yes, the idea of the transition was weighing heavily on my mind. Being a CPA, I resisted the natural temptation to do a detailed analysis of the impact of taking my income out of the household budget. I truly wanted to make a faith decision rather than a financial one. I do not recommend this approach under normal circumstances. I simply had the personal assurance of the Holy Spirit that God was going to do exceedingly and abundantly above all that I could ask or think. Further, I knew that all of our needs would be met no matter what my husband's career decision was going to be. So I took the plunge. God has been faithful to His Word and we have not missed a beat financially.

Have you taken the time to analyze your stressors? I suggest you find a quiet place where you will not be interrupted for at least 30 minutes. Make a list of every situation stressing you. Include everything from the annoying friend who competes with you to your messy, irresponsible teenager whom you love with all your heart. Now rank each one from most to least stressful. Meditate on what God would have you do in confronting these situations. You might also want to discuss some coping strategies with a trusted friend or counselor.

— TODAY'S SENTENCE PRAYER: —

Father, please give me the wisdom to deal with the things that bring pressure to bear upon me so that I may respond Your way and bring honor to Your name.

Day 2

Secure Your Foundation

*The one who hears my words and does not
put them into practice is like a man who built
a house on the ground without a foundation.
The moment the torrent struck that house, it
collapsed and its destruction was complete.*

LUKE 6:49 NIV

No structure can withstand the winds of adversity without a solid foundation. Our lives are no different. We must build them on a firm foundation if we expect to withstand the innumerable pressures of daily living.

Our lives are very similar to a stool that has a base and four legs. The base is our spiritual foundation, which consists primarily of prayer and the Word of God. The legs represent the financial, relational, mental, and physical aspects of our lives. Each leg must be strongly connected to our spiritual base in order for it to stand and be strong. Not one leg can stand alone and disconnected. For example, the financial leg must be managed according to biblical principles of giving, integrity, hard work, and so forth. If not, you will experience stressful situations, such as too much debt, bad business deals, and fiscal chaos. The relational leg must also be handled according to biblical principles or we will not have the power to exercise unconditional love, forgiveness, or long-suffering. Our mental well-being is directly proportional to the extent to which we embrace God's Word and allow it to regulate our minds and emotions—and keep us in perfect peace. A strongly connected physical leg empowers us to treat our bodies according to the principles of the Word; we get proper rest, eat right, and engage in overall health maintenance. You get the picture. The strength and success of every facet of our lives will be determined by the strength of our foundation. If the base is weak, there is no hope for the legs.

It is no wonder, then, that Satan makes every attempt to prevent us from strengthening our base. We must be diligent to secure our foundation first thing each day before we fall victim to distractions. I remember one day when I was preparing to pray. I went into my prayer room, and just as I started to pray I decided it would really be nice to listen to my sounds of nature CD that featured birds chirping, running streams, and background music. It would be a great backdrop for prayer as well as a de-stressor as I would imagine being alone with the Lord in a forest—especially if I used my noise-blocking headphones. When I went to the place where I normally kept these items, I could not find the headphones or the CD. I searched everywhere. In one room I looked through a stack of CDs that were waiting to be put back into their original cases. I figured that since I was there I'd take a quick minute to organize them. Fifteen minutes later I moved from there and proceeded to look in the trunk of my car for the missing items. There I found another array of CDs that needed to be organized and put back into their original cases. I thought, *Oh, what's an extra ten minutes? I'll make it up to the Lord.* I organized the CDs—and the entire trunk. Next I went into my home office and behold, there they were—my noise-blocking headphones and my nature CD. But since I was so close to the computer, I decided to quickly check my e-mail just in case there was one that needed an urgent reply. I have friends who jokingly describe this set of distractions as AAADD—Age Activated Attention Deficit Disorder.

Nevertheless, an hour later, I was now ready to head back to my prayer room. Of course, the hour I had scheduled to pray was up, so I ended up spending about 20 hurried, guilt-filled minutes running through my prayer list and quickly browsing through a psalm. I thought, *How rude of me to start a conversation with the Lord and then leave Him hanging for an entire hour!* Would I have done that to anyone else? Of course not. But the day was waiting and I was already behind on my to-do list. I knew that even the 20 minutes I had spent were better than nothing, but I did not feel I had really nourished my spirit. I did not feel I had made the level of connection I desired. Rather, I felt *the accuser* trying to convince me that I had only been performing an "obligatory" duty because I am "supposed" to pray because I am a Bible teacher, and teachers *should* be able to *say* that they pray consistently.

The only way I have found to be consistent in prayer is to set a specific time and place for it. Otherwise, something else will keep taking precedence over it. Do not allow yourself to be distracted. Do not fool yourself into thinking you will get to it later. By the end of the day, you'll be too tired to enter into His rest. You'll simply want to say, "God, bless everybody in the whole world. You know their needs. Good night!"

I believe a time will come in every Christian's life where the key to their survival will depend on their relationship with the Lord. When my friend Althea Sims' husband suffered a massive stroke, she suddenly found herself thrust into the role of holding together—spiritually and administratively—the church where he was pastor. She also had to assume responsibility for their household finances—a task he also handled. These were uncharted waters for her. Further, she had to continue her duties as mother to her dependent children. The doctors provided little hope of Pastor Reggie's survival during the days following his stroke. Althea was the Rock of Gibraltar and it was not a facade—you could feel her strength and her peace. Recently I asked her how she kept her sanity during that extremely stressful period. She responded, "I survived because of where I was in the Lord when it all happened." She had secured her foundation way before the storm. Solomon was right when he said, "If you fail under pressure, your strength is not very great"

(Proverbs 24:10). We cannot escape life's troubles or stressors, but we can fortify our spirits with prayer and the Word of God so that we can have the strength and courage to respond to and overcome them.

> ——— TODAY'S SENTENCE PRAYER: ———
>
> Dear Lord, please ignite in me a passion for prayer and for Your Word so that I may secure my spiritual foundation and weather the storms when they arise in my life.

Day 3

Sleep

*I will lie down in peace and sleep, for you
alone, O Lord, will keep me safe.*
Psalm 4:8

Sleep is more important to our survival than water or food. Getting sufficient sleep to restore our bodies is a key factor in coping with day-to-day stress. Further, failure to get enough sleep also increases stress and can make us less able to handle stressful situations. Most adults, regardless of age, need the recommended eight hours of restful sleep a night. But sometimes stress can keep us awake, making matters worse as we find ourselves in a vicious cycle of a stressful situation keeping us up and then a lack of sleep causing more stress. Sleeplessness, then, can be one of many signs that our body is under stress.

What about your sleep habits? Do you have a sleep routine in which you go to bed and get up about the same time, or do you allow events, people, deadlines, or other circumstances to dictate your sleep schedule? For those of you whose bedtime routine is rather extensive, do you start to wind down in plenty of time to allow yourself to complete it, or does the routine itself become a stressor? Ever thought about completing it hours before your bedtime? Most of us think of sleep as some passive process in which we drift off into oblivion and wake up several hours later well rested. The truth of the matter is that sleep is an active state. Many metabolic and other restorative processes occur during the various stages of sleep. If we do not sleep long enough for our system to be rejuvenated, we will most likely find ourselves irritated by the smallest things and battling a whale of an appetite. The excess hunger is just our body's cry for the energy that was supposed to be supplied by a good night's sleep.

If you have trouble sleeping, you can try some things to help you sleep better. Although experts say that you should not exercise within a couple of hours of turning in, I find that a leisurely walk on my treadmill helps me to sleep well. The key is not to engage in an activity that raises your heart rate significantly because that will interfere with sleep. You might also try taking a warm bath while burning an aromatherapy candle. You will want to avoid caffeine, alcohol, nicotine, and heavy meals near bedtime. (Of course, eliminating the consumption or use of these things in general would be a plus.) If you are menopausal or premenopausal, you might need to add sugar to this list. You will want to make sure that your room is dark and cool. The purchase of blackout window shades to avoid the bright morning light would be a good investment. I also use eyeshades so that the light doesn't disturb me when my husband arises before I get up. A good comfortable mattress and pillow are a must. Don't skimp here. They are as important as wearing comfortable shoes. I have one of those memory foam pillows that ensures the correct alignment of your head and body throughout the night. When I go on a trip, I notice the difference in my quality of sleep. Keep your bed linens fresh. Even if you do not change your sheets every few days, fresh pillowcases will still set the stage for a pleasant sleeping experience.

If you are unable to turn off your racing mind, try the deep breathing exercise discussed in chapter 22, "Release Your Tension." If there is an issue that you need to deal with, then plan to do so. Get in touch with why you are unable to sleep.

If none of these suggestions work and you still have trouble sleeping for three weeks or longer, talk to your doctor, a sleep disorder expert, or mental health professional. In the meantime, continue to meditate on sleep-related Scriptures, such as Proverbs 3:24: "Yes, you will lie down and your sleep will be sweet" (NKJV). And keep praying to the great Great Physician.

TODAY'S SENTENCE PRAYER:

Father, You promised to give Your children rest. Therefore, I will lie down in peace, and my sleep will be sweet.

Day 4

Nourish Your Body

*Whether therefore ye eat, or drink, or
whatsoever ye do, do all to the glory of God.*
1 Corinthians 10:31 KJV

You will be able to manage your stress much more effectively if you know how the foods you consume affect your body's ability to cope with daily pressures. Despite the many books on the market today that adequately explain how to properly fuel our bodies, nutritional ignorance seems to be the norm in America as the rate of obesity continues to rise. When the pressure is on, many find refuge and comfort in food.

Nourishing our bodies properly is a lifelong endeavor, and we would do well to become as nutrition-conscious as possible. I am surprised by the number of people who do not know the difference between proteins (lean meats, eggs, etc.) and carbohydrates (breads, pastas, potatoes, rice, etc.). Some are oblivious to the difference between *simple* carbohydrates (man-manipulated stuff, like chips, cookies, and cakes) and *complex* carbohydrates (fruit, vegetables, legumes, and foods that have not been altered by man). Complex carbohydrates and proteins are a winning combination to a healthy body and proper weight management. Finally, there are some who think that "cholesterol free" means that the cooking oils are calorie free and can be consumed in unlimited quantities versus the reality that it is simply unsaturated (won't go solid when cold) but has the same number of calories—which are the highest of all food choices. You can improve your nutritional IQ by going to your local bookstore or health food store and buying books or even pocket booklets that explain the composition of certain foods. Once you understand that there are virtually no nutrients in junk foods, you cannot in good conscience make a steady diet of them. Sure, you may crave an occasional Twinkie, but eating them regularly should not be part of your food regimen.

If you have the physical stress symptoms of poor concentration, fatigue, or a ferocious appetite, you may be tempted to get a quick fix by eating junk food. The items of choice usually contain caffeine, sugar, or something salty with a crunch. Do you find it interesting that when spelled backward, s-t-r-e-s-s-e-d is d-e-s-s-e-r-t-s? Have you noticed that you never tend to crave foods like carrots, apples, or lean meats, even though they may be better for you in the long run? But therein is the answer: the long run. It takes a healthy food choice longer to raise our blood sugar to the point where we feel satisfied, whereas the junk food delivers an immediate result because its refined ingredients are quickly assimilated. Further, they cause your brain to release serotonin, a hormone that helps you to relax—for a brief time. The time is so brief that you'll need another hit of carbohydrates to recover from the precipitous drop in your blood sugar. This time you'll probably have to consume even more carbohydrates because your blood sugar drops even lower than it was originally after the first carbohydrate fix, so your body is going to have to work harder to get your sugar level back to normal. Is this beginning to sound like a drug addiction scenario? Through all of this activity, there is a good chance that you are not really hungry, but rather feeding whatever the emotion (anger, fear, fatigue, etc.) the stress generated. A 10- to 15-minute nap may be the best solution. Of course, if you were diligent to make sure that you ate the right foods frequently throughout the day, then your blood sugar would stay at a level that would eliminate those cravings.

Learn your own body and monitor what triggers you to want to eat. One of the best strategies against stressful eating is to get the healthy protein in your system first thing in the morning. Rather than donuts and coffee, try having an egg sandwich or peanut butter and toast with low-fat or soy milk. Plan for times when you may be prone to stressful eating by having only healthy alternatives available. When I go away to write, I only stock foods that are healthy to eat. Of course, I hate it at midnight when I feel I could eat a whole bag of Oreos but only have cantaloupe available!

Nutritional and homeopathic supplements also play

a vital role in helping us to cope with stress, tension, or anxiety. However, before you begin an herbal program, you should at least make a call to your medical doctor to make sure that certain herbs do not interfere with your current medications. It is a known fact that during times of stress, more vitamin C is depleted from the body. Therefore, an extra dose to replenish it may be needed.

Our food choice habits took years to develop. I can trace my propensity to reach for sugar back to my grandmother's house, where her tea cakes made everything better when I had a problem. Now, just because I have identified the source of the bad habit does not mean I can continue to use it to justify bad behavior. It simply means I have to develop new coping habits for my life. For example, most of the time I now try to opt for a piece of fruit or a small protein bar instead of a refined carbohydrate snack that has little or no nutrients.

Prolonged stress can cause our internal systems to break down. We need to keep our insides strong by selecting foods that nourish us rather than work against us.

TODAY'S SENTENCE PRAYER:

Father, please give me the desire and the discipline to consume foods that properly nourish my body.

Day 5

Get Physical

*I discipline my body like an athlete, training it
to do what it should. Otherwise, I fear that after
preaching to others I myself might be disqualified.*

1 CORINTHIANS 9:27

Physical activity is an excellent stress-buster and is
critical to normalizing your body after a stressful event.
When your brain senses a threat or danger, it quickly
releases hormones carrying an urgent message via the
bloodstream to the adrenal glands (which sit atop the
kidneys). The message says, "Let's prepare to resist or
to run now!" The adrenal glands produce excess stress
chemicals, cortisol and adrenaline, and rushes them into
the bloodstream, where they get delivered to various
parts of the body via nerve fibers. The body responds
with increased strength, raised blood pressure, and other
assistance needed to resist or run. There have been countless stories of people who exhibited unusual strength in
a crisis. I heard of a petite young mother who actually

lifted the back of a car under which her child had been trapped.

Of course, a crisis is not limited to threats of physical danger. The threat of losing a job or a loved one, or even the excitement of a happy occasion can cause the brain to put the body on high alert. The adrenal glands do not attempt to distinguish between negative or positive excitement.

Once the crisis is over, the excess hormones need to be dissipated out of the bloodstream. This is where exercise plays a critical role. Regular physical activity helps to burn these extra chemicals so your body can return to normal. Imagine their buildup if you tend to live in a period of stress day in and day out. Studies have linked an accumulation of stress hormones to strokes, heart disease, high blood pressure, thyroid malfunction, decrease in muscle tissue, obesity, impaired memory, and a host of other maladies. In fact, people have died from heart failure in a crisis because their heart muscle was not strong enough to handle all of the stress hormones that had been pumped into the bloodstream to prepare the body to handle the crisis.

In addition to its positive impact on stress, physical activity provides us with numerous other benefits, including better resistance to illness, stronger bones, more energy, and stronger muscles. What activity is best? The best form of exercise is the one you enjoy and find the most convenient. These are the two biggest reasons why most of us fail to be consistent in following an exercise program. First, we either lose interest in the activity because we don't really get a lot of satisfaction out of doing it. I have had beginning lessons in almost every sport—two or three times for some. Rollerblading, skiing, swimming, golfing, and even completing the Los Angeles Marathon have not held my interest. I'm just a plain walker. I get great joy from bonding with my friends as we power walk or even stroll through various parks, neighborhood walking routes, and along beach paths.

Secondly, we tend to not be consistent in an activity if it requires too much time or effort to access. Why join a gym across town and only show up two or three times a year? Exercising already requires discipline, so why allow inconvenience to add more stress to the process?

Whether a brisk walk or a high-energy fitness class, almost any physical activity will help you let off steam, distract you from your source of stress, and improve your mood. It also relaxes and reenergizes your body. The duration of the exercise should be a minimum of 30 minutes of physical activity a day at least five days a week. Doing more is even better. Some fitness gurus suggest that if you cannot carve out 30 minutes at a time, grab 10-minute segments throughout the day.

There are also other benefits to making exercise the center of your stress-busting program. People who are routinely active tend to eat better, and as discussed in the previous chapter, a healthy diet also helps your body manage stress better. In addition, physical activity can help you lose weight, keep it off, and feel better about yourself. Feeling physically inadequate can be a stressor in itself.

If you cannot find the time for an official workout, try building the activity into your lifestyle. My doctor recently suggested that I park on the outskirts of the shopping mall so that I will be forced to walk farther. You may try taking the stairs several times during the day for a certain number of floors.

Stress can wear your body down mentally and physically; however, a healthy body can cope with stress better than an unhealthy one. In 1 Timothy 4:8, Paul reminded Timothy, "Physical exercise has some value, but spiritual exercise is much more important, for it promises a reward in both this life and the next."

Tailor your physical activities to your lifestyle. The most important thing is to keep moving.

Today's Sentence Prayer:

Father, I need Your divine empowerment to engage in some form of physical activity on a regular basis.

Day 6

Let Your Values Do
the Driving

*As I looked at everything I had worked so
hard to accomplish, it was all so meaningless.
It was like chasing the wind. There was
nothing really worthwhile anywhere.*

ECCLESIASTES 2:11

What are your guiding principles? What drives your behavior? Is it the quest for the finer things of life? Or maybe you are in pursuit of social status or you simply desire to achieve perfection in your endeavors. Whatever the motivation, is it worth the stress it causes you? Let's see how our Savior dealt with one woman's self-imposed stress.

One day Jesus and His disciples stopped for a visit at the home of Martha and Mary. Martha, being the consummate hostess, fretted about trying to get everything just right for her guests. Mary, however, had a different agenda. She chose to sit and listen to Jesus talk. Martha wasn't having it. She needed Mary to give her a hand, so she appealed to Jesus.

> *She came to Jesus and said, "Lord, doesn't it seem unfair to you that my sister just sits here while I do all the work? Tell her to come and help me." But the Lord said to her, "My dear Martha, you are so upset over all these details! There is really only one thing worth being concerned about. Mary has discovered it—and I won't take it away from her"* (LUKE 10:40-42).

Unfortunately for Martha, Jesus backed Mary. Mary's behavior said, "I value the opportunity to sit at the feet of Jesus and to feast on His words; therefore, that's where I'm going to invest my time and energy." This is not a story about prayer but about bringing our values and our behavior into alignment. Martha was not a bad person; she simply had misplaced values.

Values serve as our internal compass. Even corporations have developed "values-driven" principles that dictate their actions. Many post them in their hallways and common areas for all employees to see and embrace. It also keeps the corporation accountable. One very popular Christian organization has as one of its core values the importance of the family. Therefore, it is not their policy to have employees working overtime except when absolutely necessary. Their personnel policies are also family friendly.

Because our values are our internal navigation system,

when we choose a course of action that is inconsistent with these values, stress is often the result. Let's take a look at a few scripturally based values that can help to minimize the stress in our lives.

God's Sovereignty. "You saw me before I was born. Every day of my life was recorded in your book. Every moment was laid out before a single day had passed" (Psalm 139:16). We can rest in the knowledge that God has the last word on everything that concerns us. When it is all said and done, we have an ordained destiny. While God does not show us the parade of our lives from start to finish, we know that He is our drum major and we must simply march to His beat. For example, from a professional perspective, He orchestrates the timing of our promotions, our exposure to influential people, and all other aspects of our careers. It is an insult to His omnipotence when we engage in backstabbing, dirty politics, strategic maneuverings, and other stress-inducing efforts designed to advance our ball down the court. This does not mean that we shouldn't do a great job or express our desires or preferences to those who can grant them. Further, we should readily walk into a door that He opens and interact with key people He brings into our paths. It all has to do with where we put our faith—in self-efforts or in God's sovereignty.

Integrity. "The integrity of the upright guides them" (Proverbs 11:3 NIV). If we walk in integrity, we will experience the peace of knowing that we have done right in the sight of God. Integrity is not just being honest or telling the truth, but also making what you say be the truth.

You make your word your bond. When others know they can depend on you to keep your word, it eliminates their stress also. I know someone who rarely keeps his word. When he promises me something, I hardly dare to hope. In Psalm 15:4, David says that one of the traits of those who will abide in God's eternal presence is that they "keep their promises even when it hurts."

Humility. "Fear of the LORD teaches a person to be wise; humility precedes honor" (Proverbs 15:33). Humility is not a sense of unworthiness, but rather an acceptance of our God-given strengths and our God-allowed weaknesses. We rest in the knowledge of both. Our strengths should not make us proud. Our weaknesses should not make us anxious, for as God declared to the apostle Paul, "My grace is sufficient for you, for My strength is made perfect in weakness" (2 Corinthians 12:9 NKJV).

Equality. "For there is no respect of persons with God" (Romans 2:11 KJV). No person is better or more important than another. Some have simply had more access to what the world offers, achieved more education, or been called to higher levels of authority and responsibility. No one is inherently better. No one. The ground is level at the foot of the cross. No matter what our station is in life, we are to treat everyone with the same respect.

Generosity. "If you give, you will receive. Your gift will return to you in full measure, pressed down, shaken together to make room for more, and running over. Whatever measure you use in giving—large or small—it will be used to measure what is given back to you" (Luke 6:38). We are never more like God than when we give, and we can never beat Him at giving. We have no need to be anxious about not having enough if we extend generosity to others.

The list above is not exhaustive of all Christian values. Your list may include others. The important thing is that you allow your core values to become the internal force that drives your actions. To behave in any fashion inconsistent with these values will rob you of your peace.

Today's Sentence Prayer:

Father, I want You to be glorified in all I do; therefore, I ask You to give me the wisdom, the courage, and the discipline to align my decisions, behaviors, and actions with my values.

Schedule Your Day Wisely

The steps of the godly are directed by the LORD.
He delights in every detail of their lives.
PSALM 37:23

Each new day presents us with 1440 minutes to use at our discretion. If we don't consciously decide how we will spend them, we will look up and realize they passed us by without our ever starting the tasks we desired to complete. The best approach to this problem is to prepare and follow a wisely prioritized to-do list. I should warn you up front that the list itself can become a source of stress if you include too many tasks. My friend Sandra always cautions me to schedule only two or so "majors" in a day. For example, if I have to take my mother to a doctor's appointment in the afternoon, it may not be a good idea to schedule a two-hour hair appointment or other time-consuming activity that same day. I use an electronic calendar, and I categorize every activity by its importance. Contrary to the thinking of some, every activity is not equally important. You really can put off until tomorrow those insignificant things that would stress you if you were to do them today. If you are not in the habit of developing a to-do list, you may wander aimlessly throughout the day without a sense of focus. Even if you do not have a fancy personal digital assistant (PDA), a simple handwritten list will provide the same sense of accomplishment as you strike off the completed items.

Like me, many of you may be guilty of *Star Wars* thinking when it comes to scheduling your day; you think everything can be done at light speed. Consequently, you do not build in time for interruptions, lost keys, or for people who move at a snail's pace. This has caused me great stress. I used to rarely plan for extra traffic due to accidents, lane closures, and so forth. Imagine living in Los Angeles with that kind of thinking when at times you can literally read a newspaper on the freeway during rush hour traffic.

Of course, the biggest problem I used to have with my to-do list was that I often forgot to submit it to God. I prepared it the night before and printed it out so I could hit the ground running the next morning. I'm reminded of a phrase in the song "What a Friend We Have in Jesus" that says, "O what peace we often forfeit, O what needless pain we bear, all because we do not carry everything to God in prayer." I was literally giving up my right to peace by not letting God approve my schedule. What I have now learned to do is to prepare the list, hold it up to God, and say, "Lord, this is what I have in mind to do today. Nevertheless, not my will, but Yours be done."

There have been times I have scrapped the entire list and spent most of the day ministering to a friend—and the world never fell apart.

As you plan your schedule, do not plan on doing too many things at the same time. Studies have linked chronic, high-stress multitasking under intense pressure to short-term memory loss. Further, experts have concluded that multitasking actually makes a person more inefficient because it reduces the brain power needed to perform each task.

I know this to be true. I used to pride myself on my ability to juggle several tasks at once. I did not acknowledge the fact that I often had so many piles of paper, opened drawers, and unfinished chaos around me that it almost drove me crazy. Once I was cleaning the house, talking on the phone, and cooking when I heard the fire detector go off. I had started another project upstairs and had left a skillet of hot oil on the stove. The skillet was in flames and the house was filled with smoke. I was petrified. When the fire department arrived and finally cleared the smoke, I vowed to stop the multitasking—at least while cooking. Darnell has jokingly called me "Fire Marshall Bill" ever since (from the early 1990s television sitcom *In Living Color*).

When working in your office or at home, force yourself to complete a task before starting another one. This will allow you to focus 100 percent of your brain power on the selected task. I have posted a huge note on my desk that says: FINISH ONE TASK AT A TIME. It really helps me to stay focused—and productive.

Finally, if you feel you must be productive during all of your waking minutes, it's time to redefine "productive." Solitude is productive. Taking a mental time-out while waiting in line is productive. Praying for each member of your family while sitting in traffic is productive. Tightening your muscles, memorizing a Scripture (I write them on the back of my business cards), or praying for all of the souls around you to make it into God's kingdom are all productive pursuits.

Today's Sentence Prayer:

Lord, help me to remember to submit all of my tasks to You each day so that I will be productive and not forfeit the peace You desire me to have.

Master Your Money

If you are untrustworthy about worldly wealth,
who will trust you with the true riches of heaven?
LUKE 16:11

Financial friction and uncertainties are among the most frequent stressors and causes of breakdowns in relationships. Such problems are not always attributable to the fact that people do not earn enough money to cover their basic needs. As a certified public accountant, my observation has been that most people simply have not reconciled their yearnings with their earnings. My frugal father concurs. He likes to quip, "You know the best way to manage your money? Stop wanting!" The billions of dollars outstanding in consumer debt in the United States further attests to this. The masses are out of control and living in denial about their true financial status. I have heard of people who are so overwhelmed with debt that they toss their bills in the trash without even opening them.

Based upon my years of professional experience,

I'd like to offer some guidelines for minimizing your financial stress:

- Spend your money according to God's priority. Pay Him His ten percent first so that you will not feel guilty about not doing so. Disobedience and guilt are real stressors.

- Pray before you buy anything. Ask yourself, "Is this a need or a want?"

- Stay aware of your level of expenditures versus your income.

- Agree with your spouse regarding the household budget as well as your short-term and long-term goals. Do not hide or miscommunicate information regarding your finances.

- Commit to being excellent at work—without overdoing your hours.

- Pay off all consumer debt (excludes real estate). Keep one credit card for identification purposes.

- Save monthly (minimum ten percent of gross pay if you are already out of consumer debt).

- Do not cosign a loan for anyone. Do not lend a relative or personal friend money you cannot afford to lose.

- Pay cash for all of your "desires." Do not charge them.

- Always allocate funds in your budget for recreation and vacations.

- When you get a raise, do not adjust your lifestyle to consume the entire amount. Practice living beneath your means.

- Establish an emergency cash reserve of at least two months' living expenses (six would be excellent).

- Be content with what you have. Do not keep striving for more, more, more. Ecclesiastes 5:10 cautions, "Whoever loves money never has money enough; whoever loves wealth is never satisfied with his income. This too is meaningless" (NIV).

When you know you have handled your money God's way, you can relax and expect God to show Himself strong in your life. "Don't worry about anything; instead, pray about everything. Tell God what you need, and thank him for all he has done. If you do this, you will experience God's peace, which is far more wonderful than the human mind can understand. His peace will guard your hearts and minds as you live in Christ Jesus" (Philippians 4:6-7).

TODAY'S SENTENCE PRAYER:

Lord, I thank You for all of Your blessings and ask that You help me to be a good steward of my finances in every way.

Do Right

"There is no peace for the wicked," says the LORD.
ISAIAH 48:22

Sin stresses the body and robs us of our peace. It is interesting to note how a person's nervous system responds to a polygraph exam, commonly referred to as a "lie detector test." The fact is that the test cannot determine if someone is lying. It simply measures how a person's response to certain questions impacts his nervous system. God designed our system to glorify Him by conducting our lives in a holy and righteous manner. When we sin, the stress it causes negatively impacts our entire body. Even if you have never taken a polygraph exam, you can agree that when you have lied you probably experienced an increase in your heart rate.

Whenever we choose a course of action inconsistent with what we believe to be the right thing to do, stress will usually be the result. For example, because of a need for financial survival, a person may accept a job or assignment that requires him to do something contrary to his spiritual convictions, such as serving liquor or whatever else violates his conscience. For him, the thought of going to work stresses him. Many women have faced the dilemma of compromising their values in order to get a promotion or to achieve other advantages. To them it seemed to be their only option. Scripture reminds us that "there is a way that seemeth right unto a man, but the end thereof are the ways of death" (Proverbs 16:25 KJV).

Death is the ultimate separation. Compromise will stress you and separate you from the peace that comes with doing right. This is where a strong spiritual foundation is crucial. It takes faith and courage to let our convictions dictate our behavior and our choices. When Daniel, the Jewish captive who had risen to prominence in Babylon, prayed to God in violation of the king's decree, he faced the risk and ultimately the reality of being thrown in a den of lions. He placed a high premium on prayer and was willing to pay the price to maintain it as an integral part of his life. God honored his faith and shut the mouths of the lions. The king, realizing that he had been duped into signing the decree, ordered Daniel's enemies to be destroyed. Daniel continued to enjoy a long and distinguished career (Daniel 6).

You can eliminate a lot of your stress on the job by giving God the reins of your career. Yes, let management know of your desire to advance within the company, but understand that God is ultimately responsible for your progression. "For promotion cometh neither from the east, nor from the west, nor from the south. But God is

the judge: he putteth down one, and setteth up another"
(Psalm 75:6-7 KJV). Rest on this truth and focus on being
excellent and on being a team player. Obey company
policies, don't cheat in any manner, and watch God do
His thing.

Don't think you can do right in your own strength.
Sometimes the temptation to retaliate, to lie, or to advance
your ball down the court will be too much to resist if you
don't stay God-conscious. Don't stress out or give up
all hope if you fall. Learn a lesson, repent, and get back
on the wagon. Seek God daily to give you the grace to
be like Jesus. There is a line in an old hymn that says, "I
need Thee every hour." Indeed we do.

TODAY'S SENTENCE PRAYER:

Father, please keep me from falling into
temptation and please deliver me from
evil.

Enjoy the Present

*Don't worry about tomorrow,
for tomorrow will bring its own worries.
Today's trouble is enough for today.*
MATTHEW 6:34

Tomorrow is like your child. No matter whom you're with or what you're doing, it tries to demand your attention. Of course, like your child, it is very important to you and you want to make sure that you take care of it. Therefore, it would be foolish and to your detriment to ignore it. It's just that every now and then, you need a break from it.

People are so distracted these days. It seems that no one knows how to enjoy the current moment or the current phase of their lives. This can cause stress as we attempt to live in two time periods at once—the present and the future. I'm working hard on being an exception to this trend. I'm practicing being present with people from the moment they come into my presence. If you are like me, one of those hard-driving, goal-oriented types, you are going to have to learn to exercise some mental discipline in order to be present with people. One of the strategies I employ is to block enough time so that I'm not thinking of what I have to do next. I find it best to wait until I can invest more than a few minutes in being with someone so that the person is not frustrated with my divided attention and my tight schedule. (Don't use this as an excuse, but as a priority in planning your schedule.) When I visit my elderly mother, I allow at least a couple of hours or more for each visit. I take her on leisurely walks aimed as much at slowing me down as they are in helping her to exercise.

Learning to enjoy the moment requires you to focus on the person or persons you are with and what they mean to you. It is helpful to ask open-ended questions that require them to respond with more than a yes or no. Listen closely and ask follow-up questions. For example, I may ask my mother, "Who was your favorite teacher in school?" followed with another question, such as a simple "Why?" This makes people feel you are being present with them and care about their responses. Sure, your thoughts may dart into the future for a few seconds, but force them back immediately by not engaging the concern. You can deal with your future issues at another time.

Be your own "in the present policeperson" when you are having a social time with your family. Do not take phone calls. Do not use this as a time to catch up on mindless work or to process your daily mail. No multitasking allowed. If you are at a wedding, block the thoughts about the report due on Monday. Silently pray for the bride and groom. Focus, focus, focus. There is great satisfaction in doing this once you get the hang of it.

I recently took my two-year-old nephew to the Long Beach pier and found great joy in watching him run freely and discover things that are old hat to me. I policed my mind and dared it not to be present with him. Of course, with a two-year-old you don't have much choice. I did not think about publishing deadlines, upcoming speaking engagements, or any of the usual suspects that pop up when I'm socializing. King Solomon cautioned, "People should eat and drink and enjoy the fruits of their labor, for these are gifts from God" (Ecclesiastes 3:13).

Learning to enjoy the current phase of your life is an even bigger challenge, especially as it relates to financial matters. You can become so obsessed with preparing for your future that today will have completely passed without your experiencing it. So rather than musing, fretting, and wondering about the adequacy of your retirement planning, why not hire the services (it's worth it) of a financial planner who can explain what you need to do to reach your retirement goals? Once you understand and get on track with your plan, most of the uncertainty can be eliminated, and you can focus on enjoying the now.

TODAY'S SENTENCE PRAYER:

Lord, help me to remember that You are in charge of every day of my life and I do not have to sacrifice the present moment or the present period of my life obsessing over the future.

Day 11

Just Say No

I brought glory to you here on earth by
doing everything you told me to do.

JOHN 17:4

Jesus compassionately performed many miracles; however, there were times when He knew He had to move on to the next place in order to spread the gospel. Notwithstanding, sick people were still coming to Him, and His disciples were anxious for Him to heal them. On one occasion, His disciples sought for Him while He was alone praying. "When they found Him, they said to Him, 'Everyone is looking for you.' But He said to them, 'Let us go into the next towns, that I may preach there also, because for this purpose I have come forth'" (Mark 1:37-38 NKJV). Did Jesus really say no to performing additional miracles? Yes. He knew exactly what His priorities were and He stayed focused. Therefore, He was able to report to His heavenly Father at the end of life, "I brought glory to you here on earth by doing everything you told me to do" (John 17:4). Nothing more. Nothing less.

Do you find it hard to say no even when you are

being distracted from your purpose and goals? For most people, saying yes when they really wish to say no raises their stress level by several degrees. Obviously, when they do so, they are trying to avoid some potentially negative consequences, such as rejection, loss of favor, and so forth. If you find yourself faced with such a dilemma, it is a good exercise to stop for a moment and mentally play out the entire scenario of what you think will happen when you say no. The only way to overcome your fear or insecurity in this area is to start to take small risks until you are finally comfortable delivering a firm no. It eats away at your sense of self-worth to feel that you have relinquished your power of choice over to someone else. Whenever I have done this in the past, I felt angry with myself and deep resentment toward the person I could not bring myself to disappoint. I have been healed from the tendency for many years and enjoy the freedom of living with my own choices. Let's see if you can get into practice with a couple of scenarios.

Situation A: Your friend Jack has just asked you to lend him $500 until he gets on his feet. You know that Jack is financially irresponsible, and you really and truly do not want to make the loan. Plus, granting his request would cut you short on the emergency cash reserve you are building. Let's say that you tell him, "Jack, I can't do that." How do you think he will respond? How will his response affect the quality of your life thereafter? Will he pout for a while, tell all your other friends that you are stingy, or attempt to tarnish your image in some way? Do you have the emotional strength to handle any of these scenarios? Is your relationship with him so crucial to your well-being that you feel it is better to grant the loan than to bear such consequences?

Situation B: Suppose that Suzie is relocating to Beth's city and asks Beth to let her move into her apartment until she can find her own place. She knows that Beth has a spare bedroom. Beth is well aware that Suzie is quite messy. Beth tends to be a neat freak. In fact, the sight of untidiness really impacts Beth's sense of peace. Beth and Suzie have been friends for 20 years and are very close. Suzie has always been there for Beth through all Beth's ups and downs. Beth has just remodeled her place to suit her lifestyle and needs. Her extra bedroom now doubles as her office, except when she has an occasional weekend guest.

Should Beth tell Suzie no because she doesn't want to be inconvenienced? Sometimes no is not the right or godly answer for a situation. While it is good and emotionally healthy to learn to establish boundaries, we must guard against becoming selfish and unwilling to sacrifice for others. Sometimes a yes with very clear boundaries will go a long way in preserving your peace and your relationships. For example, Beth and Suzie would do well to agree upon how long Suzie will stay. Further, it is imperative that Beth communicate her quirks and druthers from how she likes the refrigerator organized to her desired curfew on a ringing telephone. I have found that a mere discussion is often not enough. I'm a firm believer in writing preferences down and reviewing them with the related party. This can be done in a lighthearted manner so that it doesn't seem so impersonal. For instance, Beth could say, "Suzie, you never know a person until you live with them, so I want to share with you some of my little quirks and eccentricities—and I'd like you to share yours as well." In addition to a commitment to the friendship, getting Suzie's preferences on the table shows consideration and fairness on Beth's part and keeps them both from having to walk on eggshells with each other.

I am amazed at the number of people who find it almost impossible to have a conversation like the one above. Trust me, it gets easier and easier the more you do it. I'd dare say that all my friends and guests know my preferences, pet peeves, and quirks. In fact, in my guest room I have a short list of preferred behavior for all who visit overnight or for an extended period of time. Some have asked me for a copy for their own use. It is not at all mean-spirited; it is merely designed to make their stay comfortable and without aggravation to us or them.

Parents are another group that would experience a lot less stress if they would just exercise some strength and stick to their guns. I have watched children test the limits just like a swimmer testing the water temperature with her feet. Children want boundaries. They need them. I have lots of nieces and nephews, and it's amazing to see the respect with which some of them respond to me versus their anything-goes parents. Spanking is not always the answer, but there should be some immediate and undesirable consequences for bad behavior.

Finally, do not be subtly manipulated into saying yes due to obvious circumstances. Some people may hint but never ask directly. If you know that your saying yes to an indirect request or supplying a need is going to be an enabling act, then look straight ahead and say, "I'll believe God with you that He will work things out." For example, my friend whom I'll call "Annie" called and asked for my prayers for her friend Sally, who has struggled financially for what seems like forever. As I queried her more about Sally's situation, it became clear to me that Annie and others have been part of the problem by always responding personally to her requests for prayer for her various financial needs. Annie did not want to face the fact that she was being manipulated. I told Annie that rather than praying for Sally, I was going to pray that God would take the scales from her own eyes so that she could see the situation for what it was and get the courage to confront and minister to Sally in a life-changing way.

"No" is a complete sentence, and it will help you lower your stress and stay sane when applied with wisdom.

TODAY'S SENTENCE PRAYER:

Lord, teach me when and how to say no when it is Your will for me to do so.

Be Flexible

*The wisdom that comes from heaven is…peace loving,
gentle at all times, and willing to yield to others.*

JAMES 3:17

Flexible people are happy people. They experience a
lot less stress than rigid types who insist on things always
being done according to policy or exactly the way they
have decided they should be done. One of the reasons
that inflexibility is so stressful is that we have to achieve
our goals and purposes through thinking humans who
often have their own bright ideas. If you are not the type
who is receptive to new ways of doing things because
you view them as a personal rejection of your own ideas,
run to the altar and get healing. Otherwise, you will find
yourself in a constant state of frustration and stress.

When I worked as a corporate manager with a large
staff that included women with children, I had to come
to grips with the fact that "life happens" and that there
would be many times when they would have to take babies
to the doctor, meet with teachers, and participate in a
host of other activities that interfered with my planned
staff meetings or the work flow. Other employees needed

to have their hours adjusted from time to time to meet family and personal demands. At first I was frustrated by all of their requests. While I always allowed them the time off, I inwardly thought, *That's a personal problem that should be worked out away from work.* However, my husband, also a corporate manager who has managed a staff that included mothers, adult children of dependent parents, single fathers, and others, convinced me to come into the real world where "life happens" and to develop a new mind-set about these realities.

Several years ago corporations realized that if they did not practice flexibility in employee work hours and even their location, they were in danger of demoralizing or losing employees who were key to their bottom line. Today they offer flextime, telecommuting, and a host of other conveniences designed to make work a win-win proposition.

Jesus was a great model of flexibility—much to the dismay of the Pharisees, the Jewish religious sect who insisted on strict adherence to the law. Once He healed a blind man on the Sabbath day. To the Pharisees, this constituted work. "Therefore some of the Pharisees said, 'This man is not from God, because He does not keep the Sabbath'" (John 9:16 NKJV). He also allowed His disciples to pluck grains from heads of wheat to eat on the Sabbath. Jesus explained His occasional easing of the "policy" this way. "Then he said to them, 'The Sabbath was made to benefit people, and not people to benefit the Sabbath'" (Mark 2:27). Can you imagine the stress level of the Pharisees as they tried to enforce every jot and tittle of the law?

How flexible are you? Are you so specific at home that your family stays on edge for fear of violating one of your endless preferences? Must the towels be folded only a certain way? If plans need to be changed due to unforeseeable circumstances, does it send you into a tailspin, or do you stop and consider that God may have a different plan for the day?

If you want to become more flexible, don't try to justify your behavior by hiding under the cloak of excellence. Yes, you'd like to see things done in the best manner possible; however, seek to understand when your behavior leaves the realm of being excellent and begins to border on being an inflexible perfectionist who not only creates stress for yourself, but for others as well.

There is a saying that some people's minds are like concrete, thoroughly mixed up and permanently set. Don't let this be your testimony. Relax. Bend a little. Try going with the flow. Release the stress of inflexibility.

TODAY'S SENTENCE PRAYER:

Lord, give me the wisdom to know when to yield to others.

Day 13

Delegate

*You're going to wear yourself out—and the
people, too. This job is too heavy a burden
for you to handle all by yourself.*

Exodus 18:18

Moses was approaching a major burnout and didn't
even see it coming. He had successfully led the children
of Israel out of Egyptian bondage and now faced the
inevitable task of managing the "people problem." He
was fully committed to getting them to the Promised
Land, and he cared about each one and their issues.
Each day he sat from morning until evening functioning
as the "Dear Abby" of the desert, mediating conflicts,
listening to the people's problems, and instructing them
in God's laws. Moses was weary of the long line, and the
people were impatient with the pace at which it moved.
Enter Jethro, Moses' father-in-law. Jethro immediately
recognized that Moses' upside-down pyramid structure,
with him on the bottom trying to bear up under all of
the problems of his people pressing down on top, was

not good for him or the people. He warned Moses that he was heading for a burnout. He suggested a plan for delegating some of the counseling tasks to a hierarchy of assistant judges, only this time with Moses sitting on top of a righted pyramid, handling only those problems that worked their way upward through the chain of command. He concluded his recommendation by saying, "If you follow this advice, and if God directs you to do so, then you will be able to endure the pressures, and all these people will go home in peace" (Exodus 18:23).

Moses' response speaks volumes about his humility and his commitment to the goal of getting the job done rather than to protecting his ego and his image as the deliverer and only problem solver. It was time to let go of some of the pressure. "Moses listened to his father-in-law's advice and followed his suggestions. He chose capable men from all over Israel and made them judges over the people. They were put in charge of groups of one thousand, one hundred, fifty, and ten. These men were constantly available to administer justice. They brought the hard cases to Moses, but they judged the smaller matters themselves" (Exodus 18:24-26). Smart move, Moses.

Are you effectively delegating the duties in your world of responsibilities? What about at home? If you have young children, are you assigning them age-appropriate tasks? My mother taught me how to cook for the entire family of nine when I was only seven years old. She often worked outside of the home and was sometimes bedridden from a chronic illness. She taught me how to make homemade biscuits, stuffing, and other recipes all from scratch. Of course, I was still a child and would often get creative with her food coloring. It was not uncommon for the family to sit down to red corn bread, pink potato salad, and other colorful but tasty dishes.

Are you training and delegating effectively on the job? When I worked in a high-level position at a Fortune 500 corporation, the unspoken rule was that you would not be promoted if you had not trained someone to take over your position. So whenever anyone was promoted, his first task was to identify and train his successor.

Let's look at a few reasons why some managers do not delegate:

- They have a "worker bee" mind-set and do not understand the real role of management in developing their employees and directing their efforts.

- Their superegos have convinced them that they are the only ones who can do the job at their required level of perfection.

- They want to retain all authority and understand that by empowering others, they must give up some of their control.

- They feel they just do not have the time to invest in the necessary hand-holding. They fail to realize that if they make the upfront investment in the important things, they will eventually stop being victims of the urgent matters.

Now let's see if there is any hope so that, like Moses,

you can learn how to improve the quality of your life by effective delegation. Here are a few delegating tips that are bound to work in your favor and decrease your stress level:

- Start with the tasks you currently perform that are basically a no-brainer for you.
- Identify someone with the capability (not just the willingness) to perform this task.
- Take the time to write out the procedures and to review them with the selected person.
- Explain why the task is necessary and its importance in the overall scheme of things.
- If the task is time sensitive, then be very clear on due dates.
- Explain your other expectations.
- Finally, review the person's progress on a periodic basis until you are satisfied that he can handle the job without your intervention. This was often an area of weakness for me. My assumption was that a smart person could do anything and do it on time. I would never check on them until the due date. The results were sometimes horrible when I realized that they were not clear on the timing or objectives. I'll always remember the admonition of Bishop Frank Stewart who cautioned, "People don't do what you *expect*, but rather what you *inspect*."

Delegating should be a win-win proposition. It makes others feel empowered and valued and it frees you up to focus on more important issues and to simply have a life. I have noticed in environments where people do not feel empowered they are more prone to working on their personal issues on company time, thus making the entire department less productive.

I believe that every manager's goal should be to assign all of his routine tasks to assistants and subordinates to the extent possible. I believe that the Jethro model still works.

TODAY'S SENTENCE PRAYER:

Lord, teach me when and how to delegate tasks to capable people when it is necessary so that I can be more effective for Your glory.

Day 14

Evaluate Your Expectations

My soul, wait thou only upon God;
for my expectation is from him.
PSALM 62:5 KJV

We all have expectations of those in our circle of inter-action—whether on the job, in the home, at church, or in our social lives. Many times we may not be totally aware of them, do not express them, or will not acknowledge that they are unrealistic. Therefore, they can cause us a great deal of frustration and therefore stress.

Consider the story of Mary and her friend Joan, who were having brunch with a group of friends one Sunday after church. Everyone was talking about the success of a project that Mary had just completed. Out of the clear blue, Joan starts a completely different conversation with the woman sitting next to her just as Mary was making a remark. Mary was annoyed by her rudeness but playfully chided, "Hey, wait a minute. We already have a conversation going here!" Joan retorted, "I don't believe in one person being the center of a conversation." Her comment really offended Mary, but to maintain her reputation for being gracious, Mary simply smiled and dropped the matter while Joan resumed her sidebar conversation. Mary could feel the increase in her heart rate as she sat there frustrated by the disrespect and inconsideration of someone who claimed to be her friend. She mentally decided to refrain from inviting Joan to any future social functions and vowed to be "too busy" for any invitations Joan extended to her.

Failed expectations will always create stress if we allow them. Mary's expectation of Joan was not an unrealistic one—unlike Donna, who becomes extremely frustrated each week when her housekeeper fails to arrange her pictures on the fireplace mantle in the exact same angle after dusting them. "All she has to do is to pay attention," she complains. "Is that too much to ask?" This really stresses Donna—especially since the housekeeper just presented her with an unjustifiable increase for her services.

In a final scenario, consider John, who worked from home. When his wife would arrive home from the office each evening, he would still be working at his computer. "Honey, I'm home!" she would yell. He would yell back "Hello" without even looking up until she came into the office where he was. It really annoyed her that he would not get up and greet her at the door. He would sometimes sense her change in mood and ask, "Is something wrong?" "Nope," she would respond while silently thinking, *He should know to get up and greet me. Do I have to teach him everything?*

The scenarios are endless. Unfortunately, some of the most harmful and stress-producing expectations are the ones we have of ourselves. "I should be able to raise three children, have dinner on the table each night, work ten-hour days, and be perfectly coiffed when my husband walks in the door." And why, may I ask, *should* you? Expectations will keep you locked into a stress-filled life in "Shoulds Prison" where everything goes and everybody behaves as he *should*.

Let's do a little exercise to put our expectations in perspective. You can start with your immediate family (spouse, children, siblings, parents) and list your key expectations of each person. Try to be objective in assessing whether they are realistic. Understand the origin or core reason for an expectation. Have you shared these expectations? If not, why not? Do you fear the parties' reactions? What is the worst that could happen? Are you willing to negotiate some of your expectations? I say *negotiate* rather than *eliminate* because in some instances you may need to continue to maintain high expectations of others or they may not have the motivation to move to another level of excellence. Notwithstanding, to preserve your peace, there may be instances in which you may have to eliminate certain expectations—especially when they involve matters of preference versus issues which are immoral or illegal.

I know a woman whose father has never said to her

"I love you," even though she says it to him at the end of each of their conversations. He simply replies, "Okay." She needs to understand that he cannot (or will not) meet her expectation because, though he does indeed love her, he is uncomfortable or emotionally incapable of saying "I love you." This is an expectation she needs to abandon.

Complete the expectation exercise for each of your key environments. What are your expectations of your boss? Do you expect him to manage your career? Do you expect your company to always be loyal to you and to never consider downsizing you out of the organization? Is this realistic? Nope. Not in today's corporations. It's not personal; it's just business. Moving along to your church, what expectations do you have of your pastor? For example, do you expect him to visit every hospitalized member of the church? This may be realistic for a 200-member congregation, but if the church's membership has now reached mega status, a visit from an assigned individual may the norm.

Please know that in order to maintain your peace of mind, you are going to have to expect less of people and more of God. Do not set yourself up to be frustrated. Bring all of your expectations before Him for evaluation. Let Him weed out the unrealistic ones. Let Him give you the courage to express the ones that need to be communicated. Trust Him to influence the hearts of those involved so that your expectations do not become a source of stress for you or for them.

TODAY'S SENTENCE PRAYER:

Father, I lay every one of my expectations at Your feet and ask that You open my eyes to the ones I should abandon and the ones I should express.

Day 15

Resolve Conflicts

*If thy brother shall trespass against thee, go and
tell him his fault between thee and him alone: if
he shall hear thee, thou hast gained thy brother.*

MATTHEW 18:15 KJV

There are few things I find more stress generating
than unresolved conflict. It keeps my adrenaline on high
alert and consumes my thoughts until I have resolved it.
Consequently, I try to confront offenses and misunderstandings right away. Not all people feel this way. Even
though Jesus commanded us to initiate a reconciliation
with an offending brother, many Christians believe that
we are to keep quiet for "peace sake." If we are going
to manage the stress in our lives, we must develop the
skills needed to address the conflicts which are sure to
arise—for conflicts are indeed inevitable. Further, the
problem with failing to confront an issue is that it is
likely to occur again.

I have set forth below some basic guidelines for

resolving conflict that, if practiced, should result in a harmonious outcome:

- Ask God to give you His words to say so that His purpose will be achieved. "My word…will not return to me empty, but will accomplish what I desire and achieve the purpose for which I sent it" (Isaiah 55:11 NIV).

- Empty your anger or other emotions out to God before engaging the offender. Emotions tend to get in the way of the facts and can hinder objective thinking. This isn't as hard as it may sound once you decide you are going to make every effort to settle the issue in a harmonious way. "If it is possible, as far as it depends on you, live at peace with everyone" (Romans 12:18 NIV).

- Be clear as to what you perceive the problem to be. Avoid vague statements that leave room for misinterpretation. For example, "You need to do better" does not really clarify the problem.

- Focus the discussion on the offender's behavior and avoid remarks about his character. For example: "It was inappropriate for you to open my private mail" is better than saying, "I can't believe you are so nosey!"

- Stay open-minded and always seek first to understand the other person's behavior rather than justifying your own. Obviously, this will require effective listening on your part. Listening will validate the other person's feelings and gives him incentive to listen to you.

- Resolve one issue at a time. Do not cloud the discussion with other unresolved matters between you. Deal with them later.

- Agree on future behavior should the situation arise again.

Strife is stressful, and it is to our advantage to keep it at bay. We cannot eliminate conflicts from our lives because we are all unique individuals with different backgrounds, communication styles, and preferences. However, we can confront the issues, resolve them, and grow as a result.

—— TODAY'S SENTENCE PRAYER: ——

Lord, help me to make every effort to live in peace with everyone.

Release the Past

*I am focusing all my energies on this one
thing: Forgetting the past and looking
forward to what lies ahead.*

Philippians 3:13

If you are battling unforgiveness, you are probably
aware of all the biblical and other reasons why you should
forgive someone who has hurt you or someone related
to you.

You probably already know that God will not forgive
you if you don't forgive an offender. "When you are
praying, first forgive anyone you are holding a grudge
against, so that your Father in heaven will forgive your
sins, too" (Mark 11:25). You already know that it would
improve your emotional and physical health if you let go
of the hurt. You realize your unforgiveness is stressing you
because it keeps the memory of the hurtful event fresh
in your mind. You may even feel your heart start to race
a little each time you rehearse the details, forcing extra
adrenaline into your bloodstream. If only the offender

could be punished in some manner, not necessarily by you, but in some way that will let him experience the pain you feel. Thoughts of retribution are your constant companions. Stop! Why are you allowing somebody to consume and control your thought life this way? Wouldn't you like the peace of mind that comes from releasing the past and focusing on your future? Let's see how you can break free from Unforgiveness Prison.

One of the most misleading myths about forgiveness is that you can pull it off in your own strength. Someone once said "forgiveness is divine." There is more to this statement than meets the eye. Forgiveness is not just a good idea; it is a divine mandate that requires divine assistance. Even the *desire* to forgive an offender is God given. "God is working in you, giving you the desire to obey him and the power to do what pleases him" (Philippians 2:13). Getting to that desire often takes years for some as they like to nurse the grudge, as a mother would a baby. It can only grow with this kind of attention. For God's children, this should not be the case because it is our desire to always do what pleases Him. Therefore, we must ask God for His intervention immediately when someone hurts us. When He gives you the desire to please Him in this regard, it is very likely that you may not feel the emotion of forgiveness. Not to worry. You have made a decision to do the right thing, and the burden is now on your heavenly Father to heal your emotions.

Let's just briefly debunk a couple of other myths about forgiveness. It doesn't mean that you have to resume a relationship with the offender—especially if it is very clear that the person is unrepentant and has not changed his behavior. It also does not mean that you are condoning what he did. You must not think you are letting him off the hook. You are simply disengaging yourself from the hook so that the hurt does not hold you back from the life that is before you. Finally, forget about forgetting. How can you forget? Only God has the capacity to obliterate events from His memory. You will always have the ability to recall the hurtful event if you choose to do so; however, God will take the sting out of it and allow you to not remember it with malice or a desire to see the wrong avenged. You must not let Satan taunt you into thinking you have not forgiven just because you still remember.

Because unforgiveness is such a big problem in the world today between individuals, as well as nations, several secular institutions are studying ways to teach people how to forgive. The Stanford University Forgiveness Project, a long-term study of the impact of forgiveness on mental health, has shown that forgiveness is supreme at reducing chronic stress—the type that eats away at you little by little over time. The researchers have asserted that the ability to forgive is learned behavior. Their methods involve convincing the participants to look for ways to extend understanding to the offender and to find something to be compassionate about. Imagine the impact if they were to introduce the "God factor."

By the way, are *you* one of the past offenders you need to release? Are you so remorseful over a past act that you are stuck and can't forgive yourself? Are you aware that whatever act you perpetrated did not catch God by surprise? Do you know that "all have sinned; all fall short of God's glorious standard" (Romans 3:23)? So why are you keeping yourself in bondage? Release yourself and live!

TODAY'S SENTENCE PRAYER:

Father God, by Your strength I release every person who has ever caused me or those whom I love any hurt or pain, and I ask for Your intervention in healing my emotional wounds.

Day 17

Take a Time-Out

*Jesus said, "Let's get away from the
crowds for a while and rest."*

MARK 6:31

God commanded the observance of the Sabbath day
for good reason: for man to rest from his labors. If He,
being supernatural, felt that He should rest after six days
of creation activity, how much more should we? Many
people today are going nonstop the way ants prepare
for the winter—with rarely a break.

Jesus was a big proponent of resting. Once He sent
His disciples on an evangelistic tour, and they came
back bursting with excitement about all of the wonderful
miracles they had performed. He responded in a manner
that we would find odd. You would think that He would
have encouraged them to keep up the momentum. Not
so. "He said unto them, Come ye yourselves apart into
a desert place, and rest a while: for there were many
coming and going, and they had no leisure so much
as to eat. And they departed into a desert place by ship

privately" (Mark 6:31-32 KJV). Does this sound like your average day in which things are so busy you rarely get a chance to take a break? Jesus was quite concerned that His disciples had no leisure. What did He know that we seem to keep missing? He never rushed around, never seemed to be stressed or controlled by the crowds, and kept His priorities straight. Jesus knew the importance rest and relaxation played in His disciples' continued effectiveness, so He insisted upon it.

In the past I have had to repent for how I abused my body by not taking regular breaks throughout the day. Why, I even bragged that I could work eight to ten hours straight without taking any break at all. I wore it like a badge of honor. I did not know then that I was stressing my joints and putting undue strain on my back. Short breaks are essential in managing stress. Longer breaks are equally critical. If your dream of a great getaway keeps getting pushed to the back burner, maybe it's time to revisit your approach to it. Why not experience it in smaller doses? Search your local newspaper or the Internet for low-cost specials. Darnell and I have committed to a weekend getaway at least once a quarter. Further, as we discussed ways for controlling our schedules, we also decided that we would leave one Saturday of each month open to do whatever we like—without a single outside obligation. We have vowed to guard this time by putting a note on our calendars that say "Do Not Book." Time-outs won't happen without a firm resolve and careful planning. You have to begin to deem your leisure time as important as any other commitment.

If you are married, you will not be doomed if you occasionally plan a short time away from your spouse. As I write this, I am on a five-day getaway in Palm Springs, California—alone. The solitude, time alone with God, and leisurely pace have really rejuvenated my mind and my spirit. Notwithstanding, it is essential that couples spend time away together to reconnect and to rekindle the fire. It is important that each spouse has a clear understanding of what to expect on the vacation so that the vacation itself doesn't become a source of stress and failed expectations. After a few disappointing trips to the snow, Darnell finally concluded that I am not the type that will be skiing down mountains or engaging in any other dangerous sports. We now agree in advance that he will probably play a few rounds of golf, will have a limited desire to shop, and will want to read a novel he has been saving for vacation. However, since we are on vacation *together,* we also agree on what activities we can enjoy as a couple, such as tandem bike riding, movies, and, of course, dinner. We even call "time-out" on certain conversations so that we can really vacate the stressors that make time away so essential.

Many pastors' wives have confided in me that their vacations are usually no fun (if they occur at all) because the pastors are constantly on the phone and never disconnect from the congregation. I wonder what Jesus would say about that!

If you are single and do not want to vacation alone, consider taking a really fun friend with you. It will surely be less expensive; however, don't let the cost be the deciding factor.

Remember that a getaway is supposed to de-stress you. It is a time of rest and relaxation for your physical and mental health, so make it a good one.

TODAY'S SENTENCE PRAYER:

Father, help me to make rest a priority in my life and to stop dishonoring my body, this temple You have given me to perform my purpose here on earth.

Day 18

Admit Your Mistakes and Shortcomings

*Confess your faults one to another, and pray
one for another, that ye may be healed.*
JAMES 5:16 KJV

"I'm sorry I was wrong." "My mistake!" "I don't know." These are words that some people find hard to say. Just the other day, I was talking to a man who blamed his former girlfriend for having his child out of wedlock and then not forcing him to have a relationship with his son for the past 25 years. "She should have put more pressure on me," he said. "I would have acknowledged him and made him a part of my life. But now look how much time has passed. Besides, she did not give him my last name." I asked him, "Is that an excuse to avoid having a relationship with him now?" It seems that everywhere you turn somebody is making an excuse for his poor choices, performance, or behavior, or failing to admit a weakness or shortcoming.

Staying blameless is a hard and stressful position to maintain. Everybody makes a mistake, misjudges an issue, or otherwise messes up something at some point. It's called being human. Oddly enough, mistakes are one of the major ways we learn. However, because of our fear of being judged negatively or losing face, we often try to cover up our mistakes—which opens the door wide for stress. On the other hand, admitting a mistake is a surefire stress-buster. It is a relief to yourself and an inspiration to others when you show the courage and the confidence to acknowledge your mistakes without defining yourself by them.

The only real tragedy about mistakes is if you don't learn anything from them. Refusing to admit a mistake closes the door for growth. Hear the words of the Lord when He admonished the Israelites to learn from their mistakes. "Jeremiah, say to the people, 'This is what the LORD says: When people fall down, don't they get up again? When they start down the wrong road and discover their mistake, don't they turn back?'" (Jeremiah 8:4).

Like Adam in the Garden of Eden, who tried to blame Eve for his eating the forbidden fruit, many people make every effort to avoid accepting personal responsibility. Circumstances and other people may have had an influence on our decisions; however, in the final analysis we are responsible for what we do. When we make a mistake, our action was our choice. Aaron made the golden calf in the wilderness because the people were getting restless about Moses' absence. However, upon his return, Moses indicted him—not the people. "He turned to Aaron. 'What did the people do to you?' he demanded. 'How did they ever make you bring such terrible sin upon them?'" (Exodus 32:21). Of course, Aaron went into a long explanation about what an evil bunch they were and how he simply collected their gold jewelry, threw it in the fire, and out came the calf. It is interesting to note that he progressed from justifying his mistake to telling a bold-faced lie. Lying adds additional stress to justifying a mistake.

The best strategy for dealing with your mistakes is to accept full responsibility, determine how not to repeat them, and move on. While this sounds simple, it is not easy. You may worry that your critics will judge you harshly, but I assure you that if you continue this pattern of dealing with mistakes, it will become easier and easier and will inspire others to emulate your behavior. What does it buy you to struggle to stay on that Blameless Pedestal? Absolutely nothing but stress. When I have found myself being unjustifiably defensive, I feel the adrenaline rush to provide the fight-or-flight energy I need to fight for my stance and to run from taking personal responsibility. On the other hand, I experience the peace of God when I admit a mistake. It relaxes me and frees my mind to focus on what to do next in dealing with the problem.

In addition to creating stress, there is another downside to an attempt to be blameless. When you deny your shortcomings and mistakes, people are likely to label you as arrogant and proud. The irony is that others connect with you better and will declare you humble when you admit your weaknesses. Humility is one of the traits that people admire most in others; pride is detested—even by other proud folks.

One of the best biblical examples of admitting a mistake is found in the account of David being unjustly pursued by King Saul. David became a fugitive and in the process unknowingly jeopardized the lives of certain priests when he asked for their help. Ahimelech the priest gave him food and a sword and inquired of God on his behalf. Doeg, King Saul's chief herdsman, witnessed the whole thing and squealed on the priest. Saul confronted Ahimelech, accused him of conspiring with David, and ordered Doeg to kill him and 85 other priests and their entire families. "Only Abiathar, one of the sons of Ahimelech, escaped and fled to David. When he told David that Saul had killed the priests of the LORD, David exclaimed, 'I knew it! When I saw Doeg there that day, I knew he would tell Saul. Now I have caused the death of all your father's family'" (1 Samuel 22:20-22). What an admission! No excuses. Just an acknowledgment that he had made a mistake in seeking their help. His next statement shows his commitment to not repeating the mistake with the remaining survivor: "Stay here with me, and I will protect you with my own life, for the same person wants to kill us both" (1 Samuel 22:23).

Humans make mistakes. They have blind spots. God is present to support our every weakness. Peace comes when we start confessing our faults to one another.

---TODAY'S SENTENCE PRAYER:---

Father, give me the strength to humble myself, to admit my mistakes, and to learn from them.

Ask for What You Want

Ye have not, because ye ask not.
JAMES 4:2 KJV

Some people know what they want and have the courage to ask for it. Others know what they do not want and have developed the skill of expressing it in a manner that does not create hostility. Both groups have learned that expressing your wishes is one of the key strategies for managing stress.

When Daniel, the Hebrew captive, was required to eat the nonkosher foods provided by his Babylonian captors, he did not stress out about what to do. "Daniel purposed in his heart that he would not defile himself with the portion of the king's meat, nor with the wine which he drank: therefore he requested of the prince of the eunuchs that he might not defile himself" (Daniel 1:8 KJV). His request was granted, and he and his three friends were permitted to eat a vegetarian diet—with great physical and intellectual success.

I recently went down to the Los Angeles whole-sale shopping district to make a few quick purchases. When I arrived, I discovered to my dismay that I had not brought my wallet, which contained my driver's license, checkbook, and credit cards. I only had a change purse and my cell phone, which incorporates various contact information. On the contact list I had included coded information for my most frequently used credit card. I knew that the chances were pretty slim that a vendor would allow me to make a purchase based solely upon the card number and expiration date—with no identification and no actual card. Los Angeles was in the midst of a record-breaking heat wave, and I greatly needed a cool but professional outfit for a very important meeting that would start in a few hours. Notwithstanding, I did not want the stress of making the trip back home to get my wallet and then returning downtown in all of the traffic. I appealed to a certain vendor to trust me. She relented, took down the credit card information, and allowed me to buy the outfit. I proceeded to the next vendor, showed him the receipt as evidence that I had already been trusted by one of his fellow vendors. He allowed me to make a purchase as well. I completed four purchases that day, including one for "cash only." God gave me favor, and I convinced reluctant vendor number three (where I shopped often) to charge my credit card for a certain amount of cash over and above the amount of my purchase in order for me to complete transaction number four. It pays to ask.

Even in more serious matters of life, if you do not

practice asking for what you want, you will live a life of frustration and resentment if you decide that people should discern your needs, preferences, or desires without your telling them. Some people daily allow others to violate their boundaries while they suffer in silence rather than asking for a change in the stressor's behavior.

Asking for what you want is probably most difficult in a work environment. Never assume that your well-being is uppermost in your boss' mind. This is not an indictment against her. She's too occupied with her own issues. If you are a salaried employee, and have been consistently working many hours of uncompensated overtime, try asking for a special bonus for a portion of the amount that it would have cost the company had they paid you for the time. Present a well-thought-out analysis, or ask for some time off equal to a portion of what the hours would convert to in terms of days. Better still, request more staff to help you do the work. Pray and decree the favor of God before you ask. If your request is denied, consider what that is telling you about the company. Of course, if the company is experiencing a financial crisis, you should understand and stick with time-off requests. Whatever you do, do not adopt a negative attitude. Keep being excellent at your work and start thinking of Plan B for your career. Sometimes management's decisions serve to motivate us to go to the next step in God's sovereign plan for our lives.

Practice expressing your boundaries or preferences in a calm, nonhostile manner. Resist the cowardly temptation to engage in hints or indirect forms of communication—at home or at work. If you are a manager and have supervisors under your charge, be clear on what you want and don't want. Phrases such as "I'd like…"; "Would you kindly…"; or "I need you to…" will go a long way in communicating your desires without making you sound hostile and demanding. Most of all, such an approach will relieve you of the stress of wondering, "When will he ever get a clue?"

One of the most unique attributes that God has given to us as humans is the ability to communicate. We do not have to stress out wishing or hoping that someone will read our minds when we could just ask for what we want.

Today's Sentence Prayer:

Father, help me to know that because You are in control of all of my relationships, I can express my needs and desires to others without fear and can trust You for the outcome.

Day 20

Limit Contact with Stress-Producing People

*If it is possible, as much as depends on
you, live peaceably with all men.*
ROMANS 12:18 NKJV

Sometimes it just isn't possible to be at peace with certain people. Acknowledging this reality, the apostle Paul in essence said, "Do all that you can to try and make it happen."

In my day-to-day interactions, I have found it best to evaluate each relationship and to prayerfully determine the extent to which I should invest my time in it. Beyond my spouse, every other relationship is subject to evaluation. Even with him I must express my annoyances and preferences or I will pay the physical and emotional price of sending unresolved anger underground. When I have a close relative who insists on always being argumentative or negative, I refuse to put myself in the position of having to interact with him on a regular basis. Holidays may be frequently enough! The same goes for friends. Those who gossip, criticize others, compete with me, or engage in put-downs will hardly ever find me available—unless the Lord urges me to spend some time with them for the impartation of His Word.

I also try to minimize my contact with people who are constantly distracted by their cell phones or other disruptions to their attention. It drains too much of my time.

We must be careful that we have not become someone's stressor. They say that people who live in glass houses should not throw stones, so I'm going to walk lightly here. I confess that I tend to stress my service providers because I will occasionally need something completed on the same day or right away. I have noticed that one of them has responded by imposing an undisclosed "rush fee."

Even a person's annoying habits can be stress producing. I have a wonderful brother who worked for more than 30 years for a popular package shipper. The company's daily delivery quota for each driver left no time for dallying. He literally ran to the door of each package recipient. It really took its toll on his health and his habits. To this day he checks his watch every few minutes. We all find his behavior stress producing and have asked him to stop it.

Another habit that stresses me is for someone to smack their lips when eating. I have prayed for years to be delivered from my irritation with this. I'm still standing in faith. Consequently, if at all possible, I avoid eating with smackers because I feel compelled to address this socially unacceptable behavior. I'll gladly join them for a walk, but dining is out of the question.

We are not commanded to spend time or interact with people who disrupt our peace. The Bible is full of admonitions to avoid people who jeopardize our tranquility. For example, King Solomon said, "Keep away from angry, short-tempered people" (Proverbs 22:24). The apostle Paul warned, "Watch out for people who cause divisions…Stay away from them" (Romans 16:17).

The next time you find yourself in the company of a stress-producing person, ask yourself these questions: Will this situation produce patience in me if I endure it rather than run away? Why does this person's action stress me? Is it because she is mirroring my behavior? Why am I choosing to continue to interact with her?

TODAY'S SENTENCE PRAYER:

Father, I need Your guidance in discerning when and how to interact with stress-producing people so that Your love always shines through me.

Day 21

Create a Peaceful Atmosphere

Peace I leave with you; my peace I give you.
I do not give to you as the world gives.
JOHN 14:27 NIV

Have you ever spent time with someone who exudes peace no matter what is going on in her environment or even in her life? I had a former coworker, whom I will call Cynthia, who suffered domestic abuse at the hands of her alcoholic husband for more than 25 years before she left him. During this time, she also lost two of her five children to violent deaths, survived breast cancer, and experienced a host of other larger-than-life problems. When I first met her I was struck by the fact that nothing seemed to ruffle her feathers. Cynthia never complained about small issues like the broken copier, the freezing temperature in the office, or even her workload as the office manager. She was the epitome of peace, and it was apparent that she was not going to let anyone take it away from her. She set the tone for her environment no matter where she was.

What about you? How much peace do you exhibit? Let's start with your job. How well do you respond to the challenges of the day in your workplace? Are you always on edge or complaining? What is the appearance of your work area? Is it neat and orderly, or are there mountains of papers all around? I'm no neat freak, but I am a lot more peaceful and proficient when I'm not surrounded by things out of place. Disorder can be mentally distracting and stress inducing. If your office is messy or you work in a space with messy people, you may find it necessary to temporarily work in a conference room or another area if you have a pressing project. If this isn't possible, try bundling papers with a giant rubber band and putting them out of sight as you work on one project at a time. Keep glass-top tables free of smudges. Live plants should be kept trimmed and free of dead or yellowing leaves. The sight of disorder can subconsciously erode your peace.

What about your overall demeanor? Are you always fuming over the mistakes of "dummies" and "idiots"? Have you learned to stop sweating the small stuff? Have you stopped to consider what a poor witness it is to not reflect peace, a fruit of the Spirit, in your life? "But when the Holy Spirit controls our lives, he will produce this kind of fruit in us: love, joy, *peace,* patience, kindness, goodness, faithfulness, gentleness, and self-control" (Galatians 5:22-23).

What about your daily commute? Do you get into your car with the intent of maintaining a peaceful atmosphere no matter what situations you encounter on the road? When was the last time you prayed for a bad or inconsiderate driver you really wished you could have given a premature trip to his eternal destination? Have you considered that you may be the only intercessor that person will have today? Do you create a peaceful atmosphere in your car by keeping the seats and floors free of clutter? Do you play relaxing music? The right music can be a great source of peace in any environment. When King Saul was tormented by an evil spirit, his servants told him, "Let us find a good musician to play the harp for you whenever the tormenting spirit is bothering you. The harp music will quiet you, and you will soon be well again" (1 Samuel 16:16).

Regarding your domestic environment, I'm going to make an assumption that no matter what goes on outside, your home is your refuge and you guard its peace with all your might. You saturate the atmosphere with prayer each day, you communicate effectively, you are far from being selfish or insisting on your way, and you and your family "let the peace that comes from Christ rule in your hearts" (Colossians 3:15).

If you are indeed a model of peace, congratulations on allowing the Holy Spirit to do His work. Stay the course. Be the light that so shines that others will look at you and desire a relationship with our Lord.

TODAY'S SENTENCE PRAYER:

Dear Lord, because You have given me Your peace, help me to know it is with me wherever I go without regard to my environment or circumstances.

Day 22

Release Your Tension

Be still, and know that I am God.
PSALM 46:10 KJV

In addition to walking, running, or other physical activities, we must practice ways to release the tension that builds up in us when we experience temporary stress. I have set forth a few strategies below that I find to be pretty effective.

Take a deep breath. I don't know about you, but sometimes when I'm working at warp speed or something is going on that threatens to stress me, I find that my breathing becomes shallow. Other times it seems I literally forget to breathe. Taking a deep breath can do wonders in diffusing the tension you may be feeling. Deep breathing relaxes you because it lowers your heart rate and circulates extra oxygen to various parts of the body. Here's the scoop on how to get the most out of it. I'm not sure where I first learned this, but I have practiced it for years. Inhale rather loudly and slowly through your nostrils (mouth closed) counting to ten. Fill your diaphragm area as if it were a balloon. Listen only to your breathing; it should sound like the ocean. Exhale slowly through your mouth, making a hissing sound with your teeth together. Listen only to your breathing. Take ten seconds to exhale. Repeat five to ten times throughout the day, depending on the amount of stress you are feeling. Obviously, this exercise has to be done in private; however, if you feel you need to do it immediately, just skip the sound effects and breathe quietly but deeply. This is also a good exercise to do when you get into bed at night. When done with the sound effects, it can be very effective in shutting down your overactive mind.

Squeeze an antistress ball or gadget. These come in several shapes. I have one shaped like a cell phone, another like a mini-calculator, and one like a tennis ball. Simply squeezing it as tightly as you'd like relieves tension. These are usually available at an office supply store.

Blow a whistle. I attended a celebration recently, and as part of the festivities all the guests received a paper funnel horn to blow at certain intervals during the program. I left the horn in my car and forgot about it. Shortly thereafter, I was driving down the street and became so exasperated with insensitive, bad drivers that I just pulled the paper horn from the side pocket of the door and blew it with all my might. What a relief! Of course, the windows were up and no one heard it except me. Any whistle will do the trick, so you might want to pick up one.

Sing. When Paul and Silas were jailed for preaching the gospel, they chose to sing. "Around midnight, Paul and Silas were praying and singing hymns to God, and the other prisoners were listening" (Acts 16:25). I have found that a nice worship song ushers me into the presence of God and floods my soul with peace.

Self-massage. Learn to massage your tense areas yourself. If you find it a little difficult to reach your shoulders and neck effectively, put a small baseball in a long sock and lean against it on a wall while holding the top of the sock with your hand. You can control the intensity of the pressure by how hard you press against the wall. This also feels great on the lower back.

These are just a few of the positive strategies you can employ in lieu of drumming your fingers, complaining, and engaging in other annoying and unproductive habits.

TODAY'S SENTENCE PRAYER:

Lord, teach me how to release the tension in my body in a way that will not dishonor You.

Laugh

A merry heart does good, like medicine.
PROVERBS 17:22 NKJV

I love to laugh. Humor has been a key stress reliever for me for as long as I can remember. In fact, many people have told me they assumed I had no problems because I always seem so happy. What they do not realize is that if I thought about it for more than a minute, I could find something to cry about each day. Rather than focusing on what isn't, I've made a conscious decision to maintain a merry heart.

"I recommend having fun, because there is nothing better for people to do in this world than to eat, drink, and enjoy life. That way they will experience some happiness along with all the hard work God gives them" (Ecclesiastes 8:15). These words of King Solomon should be taken to heart.

The impact of laughter on stress is well documented. Studies show that laughter lowers blood pressure and reduces hypertension. It reduces stress hormones and cleanses the lungs and body tissues of accumulated stale air because laughter empties more air out than it takes in. It boosts immune functions in the body. In addition to all of the preceding benefits, laughter triggers the release of endorphins—those "feel good" chemicals in the brain that make you feel joyful and elated. These are the same chemicals released when some people, after an extended period of running, experience a runner's high.

Being merry is an individual choice. No one can force anyone else to be merry by saying, "Just be happy!" When the Israelites were taken captive by the Babylonians because of their disobedience, they lost all desire to play their musical instruments. "We put away our lyres, hanging them on the branches of the willow trees. For there our captors demanded a song of us. Our tormentors requested a joyful hymn: 'Sing us one of those songs of Jerusalem'" (Psalm 137:2-3). Your ability to laugh and to be merry is often a good indicator of where you are in your relationship with God. The Israelites had lost their connection with God. "But how can we sing the songs of the Lord while in a foreign land?" (Psalm 137:4). Your stressful lifestyle can take you so far away from God that you feel you are in a foreign place spiritually and unable to laugh and to find joy in the things that once caused you to be merry.

Humorous situations surround us each day. We just have to be on the lookout for them and not ignore them. We should take advantage of every opportunity to have a good hearty laugh. I remember one morning when Darnell and I had joined hands to pray, he began by saying, "Father, we come before your groan of thrace…" I was so overcome with laughter that I could not focus on the prayer. He would not stop to allow me to regain my composure. He just kept right on praying and I kept right on laughing. I asked him later why he would not stop, and he replied, "I wasn't going to acknowledge the devil!" We still laugh about that incident today.

Swap jokes with friends. Let people know you enjoy a good laugh. Don't be shy about sharing your most embarrassing moments (let good taste prevail here). Laugh at your mistakes—especially on the job. Shed that Superwoman image and start having fun. This doesn't mean you have relaxed your standards for excellence. It just indicates you are aware of the fact that you and those around you are human. So have fun. Be a good sport. When others do imitations of you, laugh and pay attention. That can be a real eye-opener to some of your eccentric ways.

I should caution you to be careful in teasing others. It is not wise to have a laugh at someone else's expense by making them the butt of a joke. Some people are extremely sensitive and insecure, so make note of them and veer toward the fun people.

Don't allow life's pressures and negative circumstances to snuff out your sense of humor. Laughter reflects positive emotions and makes you a lot more fun to be around. Nobody enjoys a sourpuss. Laughter can also take your mind off of what's stressing you. Laugh often, "for the joy of the LORD is your strength!" (Nehemiah 8:10).

TODAY'S SENTENCE PRAYER:

Father, Your joy is my strength, so please help me to enjoy humor and laughter throughout the day.

have to wait; they punch the elevator button repeatedly to make the elevator come faster; they click their writing pens to the point of making those around them want to go berserk. These people remind me of hummingbirds. These tiny birds can fly forward and also hover in midair going nowhere. Their tiny wings can move up to 75 times each second! The average life span of a hummingbird is only three years. I cannot help but compare them to the eagle. Eagles live an average of 30 years. Rather than excessive wing flapping, they soar. They can stay aloft for hours flowing with the wind currents. Eagles can be spotted at altitudes of 10,000 feet. When we stop rushing and start soaring with the wind of the Holy Spirit, like the eagle, we will last a lot longer and go much higher than we ever dreamed.

I realized how my "hurry habit" was affecting my family one day when I called from an out of town trip to speak to my five-year-old niece. When my brother called her to the phone, I heard him say, "Hurry! It's Auntie Deborah." The truth of the matter was that I was *not* in a hurry and had set time aside to talk to her for as long as she liked. However, I had developed a reputation for scheduling every moment of the day and for only having a limited time for every activity. Most people assumed that when I called, they needed to expedite the conversation. I was really taken aback because I knew I had earned this reputation. I did indeed have a hard time dealing with people who talked or moved slowly. When I interacted with them, I tried to speed them up by talking or moving faster—hoping they would emulate my behavior. I would deliberately answer my phone at home and at work with a "hello" that sounded as though I were rushing to put out a fire. Getting the hint, most callers would go into high gear to get to the point. My husband told me to stop answering the phone if I did not have time to talk. He said it was a put off to others. A few close friends confirmed his assessment.

Have you considered the possibility that your pace may be stressing others? If you are the impatient type that tends to move faster than most, there is a good chance you cause others to interact with you at a speed outside their comfort zone. For them, this spells stress. Now, in your defense, I submit that your job may have played a role in your developing this behavior. If you find that you always seem to be in a hurry mode and you have done everything within your power to fix the situation, such as proper staffing, effective delegation, and good time management, then it may be time to seek God's will regarding a change of employment. Is it really worth your life? Isn't a quality life at the core of why you work?

Know that every time you get into a hurry mode you send a "state of emergency" signal to your body. It responds by releasing the stress hormones adrenaline and cortisol that prepare you to deal with danger. The body cannot distinguish between physical danger, the danger of losing your job, or any other form of pressure being brought to bear. It only knows that action has to be taken and that it must energize you to deal with it. Now, this is a good thing if you are indeed physically threatened, but to live with your body always on high alert is like fighting a 15-round nonstop boxing match. You will eventually pay the price in the form of heart disease, high cholesterol, ulcers, forgetfulness, and a host of other conditions.

What is the cure for the hurry habit? It's as simple as A-B-C: Awareness, Belief, and Change. Become *aware* of your constant high-gear mode and what role you play in each instance of your hurrying. Ask yourself, "How could I have avoided this?" *Believe* that the Holy Spirit can and will give you the victory if you ask Him. *Change* your behavior. Consciously start to slow down. Talk slower. Move slower. Heed the adage that "haste makes waste." Haste causes duplication of work, accidents, and other perils that result in more lost time. My incidents of "haste makes waste" are legion. They have ranged from finding the cordless phone receiver in the refrigerator to running over my laptop computer that I thought I had put in the trunk of my car. Further, I used to talk so fast that in my conversations with others, they constantly asked me to repeat what I had said. I found this so frustrating and would silently scold them by thinking, *Just listen faster, Snail!* I enrolled in a speech class designed to cure my problem. The instructor required me to read a short passage of text in a very deliberate manner and to slowly pronounce each syllable of each word. The selection had to be stretched for a minimum number of minutes. If I finished it too quickly, I had to repeat it. It helped me tremendously. This is a good exercise to practice at home if you are a speed talker. You could start by reading a page of material at your regular pace. Note how much time it required. Then, try taking twice as long reading the same material. I found it helpful to tape my session with a small recorder. Nevertheless, I frequently revert to my speed-talking ways when I get excited. Whenever I speak in public, I usually assign someone the task of signaling me if my speech has gone into warp speed.

Deciding to move at a slower pace will definitely improve the quality of your life. Don't try it alone. God wants to help you. "Be still, and know that I am God" (Psalm 46:10 KJV).

TODAY'S SENTENCE PRAYER:

Lord, help me to operate at a pace that will allow me to enjoy and savor each moment of the day You have given me.

Solidify Your
Support System

*A friend is always loyal, and a brother
is born to help in time of need.*

PROVERBS 17:17

No man is an island. No man stands alone. Just as
God created our physical bodies in such a way that our
various internal systems support each other, so it is in
our relationships. Everybody needs a support system.
Many times, when a person's pride is working overtime,
or when he has experienced what he feels is an unforgiv-
able hurt at the hands of friends, family members, or
his church family, he will decide to write off the whole
human race and try to go it alone. "It's just going to be
God and me from now on," he may declare. Big mistake!
No one should attempt to deal with the pressures of
life in isolation. I believe that isolation is one of Satan's
most effective strategies. He has a clear shot when there
is no one to help you block his fiery darts. "A person

standing alone can be attacked and defeated, but two can stand back-to-back and conquer. Three are even better, for a triple-braided cord is not easily broken" (Ecclesiastes 4:12).

I knew a young lady who had a baby out of wedlock. She also had a very demanding job. Unfortunately, she had no support system. She did not have a warm and friendly personality, rarely extended herself to others, and had not invested in the kind of relationships where people were aware of and willing to help her when problems arose. She often found herself in a dilemma when her child needed to be picked up from day care or required other special attention at times that she was not able to get off from work. King Solomon admonished, "A man who has friends must himself be friendly" (Proverbs 18:24 NKJV).

I know firsthand the value and benefit of support when one is under stress. Not only do I have a supportive husband, but I also come from a large family who will come to my rescue at the drop of a hat. Beyond just having someone to commiserate with about the problem, it is great to know they care about the outcome. Study after study has shown that people who have caring support live longer, recover from illnesses faster, and find life more meaningful. Support gives us a sense of connection and acceptance that are core human needs. Support provides an arena in which you can be vulnerable, a place where you can feel safe in saying "I don't know," "Can you help me?" and "I need a hug." This is support God's way.

In an ideal world, our primary support would come

from our family. However, if this is not your reality, don't despair and don't get stuck wishing it were so. God has made provision for you through church fellowship groups, people with common sports or professional interests, coworkers, and other groups. You must take the initiative in reaching out and establishing meaningful relationships.

As you seek to solidify your support system, keep in mind that support must be mutual. "Share each other's troubles and problems, and in this way obey the law of Christ" (Galatians 6:2). Nothing is more detrimental to a support system than for it to become one-sided. Don't become so engulfed in your own issues that you forget your supporters are also dealing with the pressures of life. Inquire about and genuinely listen to their concerns. Nobody likes a taker. I had a friend who absolutely could not listen to my issues for more than a few minutes before she would interrupt and turn the conversation into an endless discussion of her problems. I pointed out to her several times her tendency to do this, but she never changed. It was so frustrating. I finally became "too busy" to continue the relationship.

Finally, do not forget to express tangible appreciation for those who support you. Cards and token gifts on special occasions go a long way in saying "I acknowledge and appreciate your help." Don't allow your support system to fall apart because of lack of nourishment on your part. God doesn't want you to walk on the dangerous ground of isolation.

TODAY'S SENTENCE PRAYER:

Lord, thank You for the people You have put in my life to support me and for those You have ordained for me to support in their time of need.

Stop Stress-Speak

You are snared by the words of your mouth;
you are taken by the words of your mouth.
PROVERBS 6:2 NKJV

Do you realize how often you program yourself for stress by the words or phrases you use to describe simple activities that do not necessarily need to be done quickly? In this chapter, I want you to become sensitive to your stress-oriented vocabulary. I hope you will find alternate ways of describing your actions so that you are not snared into a stress-mode by the words of your mouth. Consider the examples below:

> *Stress-oriented:* "I have to run to the store."
> *Alternative:* "I'm going to the store."
>
> *Stress-oriented:* "Let's grab a bite to eat."
> *Alternative:* "Let's have lunch."
>
> *Stress-oriented:* "I'm going to jump in the shower."
> *Alternative:* "I'm going to take a shower."

Stress-oriented:	"I'm going to throw the clothes in the dryer.
Alternative:	"I'm going to put the clothes in the dryer."
Stress-oriented:	"I'll swoop by and pick up Jane for the party."
Alternative:	"I'll pick up Jane for the party."
Stress-oriented:	"I'll be back in a flash."
Alternative:	"I'll be back shortly."
Stress-oriented:	"I'll hurry over before the game starts."
Alternative:	"I'll be over before the game starts."
Stress-oriented:	"I'm going to zip through this part of the report."
Alternative:	"I'm going to cover this section briefly."

All of these stress-oriented phrases imply a sense of urgency that sends a message to your body to get the adrenaline pumping.

Even if we do not initiate the rush vocabulary, we are still surrounded with rush messages from all forms of the media. There is a popular television commercial that exhorts customers to "Run, don't walk!" to their upcoming sale.

You may have other phrases, in addition to the ones above, that you are in the habit of using. On your road to stressing less, why not become conscious of how you describe your activities? Catch yourself in action and start reprogramming your vocabulary.

Further, I will challenge you to try to stop using the word "stress" or "stressed out" when describing your situation. Since stress affects your mind and your body, why send an unnecessary alarm to them? If you have many pressures that are being brought to bear upon you, rather than saying "I'm stressed out," try saying "I am working through several projects and personal issues right now. I know that the Holy Spirit is going to help me to get through them all."

Just recently I had to complete 80 hours of continuing professional education credits within a two-week period and was also faced with a publishing deadline with the same due date. Rather than focusing on the potential stress this was sure to cause, I started looking for quick solutions. I found a few self-study courses and completed the continuing education task within a week. Further, I asked for and was granted a 30-day extension on the publishing deadline.

If you are faced with deadlines and other pressures, stay solution oriented. Most importantly, ask God for His intervention. "In all your ways acknowledge Him, and He shall direct your paths" (Proverbs 3:6 NKJV).

—— TODAY'S SENTENCE PRAYER: ——

Lord, please help me to be conscious of those times when my words program me for stress.

Deal with Disappointments

Many are the plans in a man's heart, but
it is the LORD's purpose that prevails.
PROVERBS 19:21 NIV

During my senior year of college, I became engaged to a young man whom I'll call Tom. I had visions of us both climbing the corporate ladder and living happily ever after. He was a rising star in a Fortune 500 corporation, handsome, and a Christian. However, like Naaman the leper in 2 Kings 5, he had a proverbial spot: He was extremely jealous. He did not even want my own mother to buy me a gift. At first I found his devotion to me endearing. Then I began to see that he had taken it to the extreme because of his insecurity. Things came to a head when I visited my mother in Los Angeles during my last summer of college. During my stay, I also paid a visit to his uncle, who turned out to be very flirtatious. When he made a pass at me, I rebuffed him. To retaliate, he called my fiancé and accused me of having an affair with someone. Tom believed every word—as a typical insecure person would. He was so upset that he broke off our relationship. I felt as though the end of the world had come.

After graduation, I immediately moved to Los Angeles. I prayed to be reconciled with Tom for almost a year. I did everything I had heard faith ministers teach. I claimed Tom as my husband. I reclaimed him daily. God said no, but I wasn't having it. I was convinced that Satan was holding up my blessing. I kept petitioning God. "Does not Your word say that You will give me the desires of my heart? Is that deal still on?" "And what about Mark 11:24? Doesn't it say that whatever I ask for, if I believe that I'll receive it, I'll have it?" God seemed to dig His heels in and kept saying no. I finally accepted the fact that it just wasn't going to happen and moved on with my life. About seven years later, I met my husband, Darnell, who is one of the most secure men on the planet. I thank God to this day that He did not answer my prayer to be reunited with Tom. I would have been miserable! It was through this emotional storm and many others since then that I have learned the truth of Romans 8:28: "We know that God causes everything to work together for the good of those who love God and are called according to his purpose for them."

I have seen many women forge ahead to solidify a relationship in which God had thrown up a zillion red flags—and they rationalized away each one. The disappointment that sets in after the marriage is sure to generate a great deal of stress.

I have concluded that the first three letters of the word

disappointment are an acronym for Divinely Initiated Stop. Since disappointment is in essence the death of a plan, our best response is to grieve it and move on. Now, I don't mean to make this sound simplistic, but trying to work outside of God's will is like trying to dig your way through a brick wall with a fork. Rather than digging your way out of prison, you will dig yourself into one when you insist on getting what you want. It can be debilitating and stress producing to make attempt after attempt to get the desired thing to come to fruition. Each day I am practicing not allowing myself to get stuck in a disappointment ditch for very long. "The Lord Almighty has spoken—who can change his plans? When his hand moves, who can stop him?" (Isaiah 14:27).

Do you really want to pursue a plan God has not ordained? Can you trust Him enough to know what is best for you? Don't stress out over what should have been. If God had ordained it, it would have happened. If He has not, run the other way.

TODAY'S SENTENCE PRAYER:

Lord, according to Jeremiah 29:11, Your plan for me is to prosper me and to give me hope and a future; therefore, please help me to want only what You want for my life.

Change Self-Sabotaging Behavior

*A prudent person foresees the danger ahead
and takes precautions. The simpleton goes
blindly on and suffers the consequences.*

PROVERBS 27:12

Are you your own worst enemy—your biggest stressor? Do you engage in behavior that often leads to a stress-producing incident? Listed below are several behaviors or situations that you would do well to consider eliminating from your daily routine:

- Some women carry large purses that contain everything that they will need from sunrise to sunset. Trying to locate an item in it—particularly in a rush—can be quite stressful. To break the "everything but the kitchen sink" habit, note how often you actually use each item in your purse each day. If the answer is never, then it may be a good candidate for leaving at home. Try carrying only the basics, such as your wallet, lipstick, and keys.

- Do you find yourself driving down the freeway and fumbling for your cell phone when you get a call? Why not just make a habit of putting the phone in an easily accessible spot the minute you get in the car?

- Do you shop with your purse open as if to say to a would-be purse snatcher, "Welcome. Come on in"? Further, an open purse allows items to fall out of it. I live in a hilly area, and I'm always spilling the contents of my purse when I go down the hills. This is frustrating, but whom can I blame for self-sabotage?

- How peaceful are your travel preparations? Because I travel a lot, I keep duplicate items of toiletries packed in my suitcase, and therefore have no need to run around looking for them at the last minute. In the past, I have forgotten almost every item at one time or another that I considered "essential." Now, I have a preprinted packing checklist that sets forth everything I will need. I print out a copy for each trip. The list is categorized by business, personal grooming, exercise gear, books/products, and so forth. It has made getting out of the house for my trips a lot less stressful.

- How many times have you lost your car in a parking lot or structure? Wherever I park now, the first thing I note is my parking location. I recite it several times as I leave the car. I once was only minutes away from reporting my car stolen after having looked for it for what seemed like hours. I finally located it on a floor of the parking structure where most of the cars had left. No more of this stressful madness for me.

- If you've entered that forgetful period in your life, when you go out, look around you when you get up to be sure you've collected all your belongings. Constantly losing your items can cause quite a bit of stress for you and your companions.

- At home, always have a designated place for the things you need to use often. I keep a bowl or a basket by the door for keys, a vitamin carousel that stays in a set place, a closet organized in a manner such that the things I can wear currently are positioned in the front to avoid my going through the entire closet each time I have to get dressed.

- Do not take the cordless phone from the room where the base is located. It may be worth your sanity to have a phone in each room.

- If you wear reading glasses but can't keep up with them, buy several pairs and designate each one for a particular location. Be diligent to keep them in their appointed places.

- Do you realistically plan for traffic or things not going as scheduled? Are your assumptions too optimistic as to how long it will take to complete a task or drive to an appointment? The truth of the matter is that I could indeed do things within the bounds of my optimistic time frame if I were the only person on the planet. However, things happen. Rather than bemoaning certain realities, you simply need to anticipate them.

Try to reduce most of your daily activities to a routine. Good planning and forethought are critical to minimizing self-caused stress. They will not reduce you to a life of boredom but rather will give you more time to plan something exciting and fulfilling.

TODAY'S SENTENCE PRAYER:

Father, please help me to anticipate and make provisions for situations that could be stress producing.

Day 29

Understand Your Sphere of Influence

*And which of you by worrying can add one
cubit to his stature? If you then are not able to
do the least, why are you anxious for the rest?*
LUKE 12:25-26 NKJV

"The armies are coming! The armies are coming!"
This was the essence of the message that caused fear to
grip King Jehoshaphat's heart. The messenger reported
that three nations had joined forces and were coming to
invade his territory. Talk about pressure! His response to
this imminent threat is an example that we can all emulate
when faced with situations that seem to overwhelm us.
I call it the Jehoshaphat S.T.R.E.S.S Model. The story is
related in 2 Chronicles 20.

S—Seek God's Guidance: "And Jehoshaphat feared,
and set himself to seek the LORD" (verse 3 NKJV). Many

years prior when his father, King Asa, had faced a threat from formidable enemies, he had responded by immediately gathering the silver and gold from the temple and from his palace and using it to bribe one of the invading kings to defect to his side. That solved the immediate problem—however, not without great consequence. Although the invasion attempt was abandoned, God became angry at King Asa's reliance on another king to help him defeat his enemies (see 2 Chronicles 16:1-9). God pronounced Asa's punishment for the rest of his reign: "In this you have done foolishly; therefore from now on you shall have wars" (2 Chronicles 16:9 NKJV). He would live with the stress of always being at war because he had not sought God's counsel first. King Jehoshaphat was not going to follow the path of his father. His immediate response was to seek God's guidance.

What about you? Do you stress out trying to figure out a solution to a situation instead of determining how God would have you handle it? Think of the last dilemma you faced. Did you rely on the opinion of your friends or your self-generated ideas, or was your first thought to seek God?

T—Trust What He Tells You to Do: " 'You will not need to fight in this battle. Position yourselves, stand still and see the salvation of the LORD, who is with you, O Judah and Jerusalem!' Do not fear or be dismayed; tomorrow go out against them, for the LORD is with you" (verse 17 NKJV). God's way of resolving our issues can often go against our logic. Perhaps that is why we are often reluctant to approach Him in certain matters. Why would God instruct the army of Jehoshaphat, which was obviously no match for three armies, to show up prepared for a battle they were not expected to fight? That made no sense! Nevertheless, God will often tell us to "position" ourselves to deal with a difficult task or problem we feel totally inadequate to confront. Our challenge is to obey and "position" ourselves for victory.

"But," you may ask, "how do I do that?" Let me give you some examples:

- You "position" yourself when you decide to enter college, even though you may not have done well in high school.

- You "position" yourself when you quit your job at God's urging and start that new business, even though there isn't a long list of customers or clients waiting in the wings.

- You "position" yourself when you sit down to write that book you have always wanted to write by showing up at the computer each day—not with a head full of knowledge, but a heart full of faith that God will meet you there with His words.

God's instruction is to position ourselves to succeed. He just wants us to show up so that He can show Himself strong on our behalf.

R—Remember Past Victories: "Are You not our God, who drove out the inhabitants of this land before Your people Israel, and gave it to the descendants of Abraham Your friend forever?" (verse 7 NKJV). If God has worked a miracle for you or anyone else in the past, He can do it again. Take faith from recalling His great deeds.

E—Exalt God Above the Problem: "O Lord God of our fathers, are You not God in heaven, and do You not rule over all the kingdoms of the nations, and in Your hand is there not power and might, so that no one is able to withstand You?" (verse 6 NKJV). In his distress, Jehoshaphat asked rhetorical questions that decreed how big his God was compared to the problem. Sometimes it's hard to look beyond the problem when the reality of it is so close. It is like putting a coin over each eye—it can totally blind you to all that is before you. For every stressful situation, we must remember the words of our heavenly Father, "Behold, I am the Lord, the God of all flesh: is there any thing too hard for me?" (Jeremiah 32:27 KJV).

S—Solicit the Prayers and Support of Others: "Jehoshaphat…proclaimed a fast throughout all Judah. So Judah gathered together to ask help from the Lord; and from all the cities of Judah they came to seek the Lord" (verses 3-4 NKJV). Here was a leader who understood that he was not the Lone Ranger and that he needed the spiritual power that comes with unified fasting and prayer. He did not hesitate to ask for it. Neither should we. This is not asking for opinions, but for intercession that moves the heart of God.

S—Stand on the Promises of God: "So they rose early in the morning and went out into the Wilderness of Tekoa; and as they went out, Jehoshaphat stood and said, 'Hear me, O Judah and you inhabitants of Jerusalem:

Believe in the LORD your God and you shall be established; believe His prophets, and you shall prosper'" (verse 20 NKJV). I can never say too much about the power of hiding God's Word in our hearts so that when we need it, we can readily access and stand on it. When we do so, we can say like the psalmist, "As pressure and stress bear down on me, I find joy in your commands" (Psalm 119:143).

Finally, we would do well to recognize that like Jehoshaphat, we all sometimes face situations of varying degrees that are outside of our area of direct influence or control. The truth of the matter is that we really don't control anything anyway—especially situations that relate to other people's behavior. The fact that God may have used us to pray for, counsel with, or otherwise persuade someone to pursue a certain course of action should not lead us to conclude that we can control him. We were just instruments in God's hands. Only God can change a person's mind. I have several friends who constantly complain about how they are tired of trying to get their irresponsible children, husbands, or other relatives on the right track. They have failed to realize that the issues that are within their circle of concern are not always in their circle of direct influence. They need to let go of the stress of trying to achieve what only God can do. Their wisest action would be to continue to intercede for God to change the person or to change them.

---- TODAY'S SENTENCE PRAYER: ----

Dear Lord, help me to know the difference between my circle of concern and my circle of influence and to always seek Your guidance first in every stressful situation.

Maintain a Positive Outlook

Abraham never wavered in believing God's
promise. In fact, his faith grew stronger,
and in this he brought glory to God.

ROMANS 4:20

I lost the keys to my car today. I attended a luncheon in downtown Los Angeles and decided to meet my friend Yvonne at her office and ride with her. After the luncheon, I assumed that my keys were in my purse when we left the hotel. Once I realized that they were lost, I remember thinking, "If only I had followed my own advice!" In chapter 28 I advised that anytime you go out, it is wise to look around you before you leave the area where you have been sitting to be sure that you have collected all of your belongings. I didn't do that. I was particularly concerned about the lost keys because the car's ignition key was the type that had to be ordered from the manufacturer at a very exorbitant price. I resisted the temptation to succumb to a negative attitude regarding whether or not I would get the keys back. I refused to envision myself writing the check for the replacement key. I also reminded myself that God was fully aware of the fact that I had a critical doctor's appointment in the next hour and could not be late for it. Most importantly, God knew exactly where those keys were; nothing is ever hidden from Him. After much searching, phone calls, and prayer, the hotel staff located the keys. All ended well.

This incident may pale in comparison to the challenge you may be facing; however, the principle of Romans 8:28 is always the same: God works things out on our behalf when we love Him and are called according to His purpose. He is just as concerned about lost keys as He is about insufficient funds, troubled relationships, terminal illnesses, or any other of life's challenges.

Maintaining a positive outlook requires not only faith, but also mental discipline. While you may believe that God is in control of your life, oftentimes the reality of a situation can overwhelm your mind and threaten to negate your faith. In times like these, it pays to have developed the habit of "casting down imaginations, and every high thing that exalteth itself against the knowledge of God, and bringing into captivity every thought to the obedience of Christ" (2 Corinthians 10:5 KJV). As you arrest those negative thoughts, "fix your thoughts on what is true and honorable and right. Think about things that are pure and lovely and admirable. Think about things that are excellent and worthy of praise" (Philippians 4:8).

The amount of stress you experience in a situation will

be determined by your attitude toward what is happening. If you start confessing that you are overwhelmed, then you will experience what you have heard, for faith comes by hearing. On the other hand, if you maintain that God is in control and that you will prevail, indeed you will. Begin to act as your own "attitude policeperson." Start to notice how you respond to long lines, undesirable weather, impossible relatives, or other would-be negative situations. Do not justify your behavior. To be associated with Christ is to be positive; it is a result of being filled with the Spirit of God. There should be no such thing as a "pessimistic Christian" any more than there is "cold hot sauce." What's in us gives us our flavor.

If you find that your attitude tends to lean toward the negative, try the following to get you on the road to a better mind-set:

- Watch the company you have been keeping. Attitudes are contagious.

- Regularly read the miracles of the Bible and the exploits of men and women of faith.

- Prayerfully consider a change if your church does not adequately emphasize a life of faith.

- Know that pessimism is an insult to your omnipotent Father. It is an indication of your lack of faith in Him to make matters better.

- Consider how your attitude impacts your witness for Christ.

A positive attitude will not only minimize how much

stress affects you, but also has a direct correlation to how our bodies respond to diseases. Numerous studies have shown that optimistic people who are diagnosed with terminal illness tend to live way beyond the normal predicted life span. "A relaxed attitude lengthens life" (Proverbs 14:30).

TODAY'S SENTENCE PRAYER:

Lord, help me to reject all negativity and to become an eternal optimist for Your glory.

Epilogue

Stress is the disease of this century. Nobody escapes its presence. It can be compared to the weather. When the weatherman predicts rain, it's not just for a certain group of people. Everyone will experience it. However, there will be some who will be smart enough to prepare for it by having their umbrellas and raincoats with them. Their experience will not be the same as those who were not prepared. That's the point I have tried to get across in this book—to get you to understand how to prepare for and handle life's stressors so that you will not find yourself soaked and drowning under their weight. In Matthew 11:28-30, Jesus gave us hope: "Come to me, all of you who are weary and carry heavy burdens, and I will give you rest. Take my yoke upon you. Let me teach you, because I am humble and gentle, and you will find rest for your souls. For my yoke fits perfectly, and the burden I give you is light." Today's stressors are too great and too numerous for you to try to handle in your own strength. Peace is still possible if you will do things God's way.

Don't be afraid to make the transitions God may tell you to make so that you can exit the stress highway. His way is going to be much easier than your way. Put every area of your life under the microscope. Hear what the Spirit is saying to you. Remember that *you* control your calendar. Every appointment reflects a decision *you* made.

My computer program malfunctioned recently and the problem was affecting every document I typed. Despite my best efforts, I could not get it to operate properly. When I called the technical support hotline, the technician directed me to a file on my computer called "Normal." He then instructed me to rename it and call it "Normal B." He explained that the old normal was corrupt and that we had to create a "new normal" by establishing new procedures. You may be keenly aware that your old stress-generating behaviors are corrupt. It's time to establish a new normal.

Stress takes a quiet toll. It may take years to show up. You cannot run on full throttle indefinitely without impact. It is not God's best; it is not His will. Be honest about your stressors and don't try to rationalize them away. Know when you are being your own worst enemy and are sabotaging your own peace.

I have enjoyed a great deal of peace starting from the time I fully committed my life to the Lord more than 35 years ago. During the process of writing this book, I finely tuned my coping strategies. I have a new appreciation for solitude since I left my high-stress job. I interact with my brothers more and allow them to use me as a sounding board, and I plant the Word of God during each conversation. I pray for discourteous drivers. I don't increase my driving speed if I'm late to an appointment. I practice deep breathing several times during the day. I still tend to rev up more than I desire; I am a high-strung person who loves life. I want to do everything—now. However, I've come a long way in tempering my schedule to reflect a load that Jesus would approve. I now understand why I must exercise regularly, which is a relaxation response in order to counter the stress hormones released into my bloodstream throughout the day, even if the source of the stress is a positive event.

I find myself feeling burdened for those who wear their overloaded schedules like a badge of honor. I know that they are a ticking time bomb that may one day explode.

I encourage you to continue to read stress-related materials and to educate yourself on the impact stress has on the body and the ways to combat its ravages. Freely share the information with those in your circle of concern.

If you arm yourself against stress by putting into action the principles, strategies, and recommendations in this book, you will add years to your life and life to your years!

Appendix A

The Worry-Less Daily Assessment Checklist

Review the list of questions below daily. For each "No" response, go back and review the respective chapter in which the question was discussed. Meditate on the related Scripture and the short sentence prayer.

1. Did I take the time to become clear on the nature and core reason why a certain situation threatens to stress me today?

2. Did I strengthen my spiritual foundation by connecting with God through prayer, Bible reading, and meditation?

3. Did I sleep at least seven to eight hours the night before?

4. Did I avoid foods that provided no nourishment?

5. Did I engage in a physical activity for at least 20 to 30 minutes?

6. Did my actions align with my core values relative to God, family, etc.?

7. Did I schedule my day to include only a few versus numerous major tasks?

8. Did I spend within my budget?

9. Did I resist the temptation to do wrong in any way?

10. Did I make an effort to enjoy today rather than focusing totally on the future?

11. Did I say no to a request that would have distracted me from my goal or purpose?

12. Did I exhibit flexibility, even though I wanted things done my way?

13. Did I delegate a task rather than doing it myself?

14. Did I evaluate my expectations when someone frustrated me?

15. Did I attempt to resolve a conflict today by running away, exploding, or handling it God's way?

16. Did I make a decision to forgive and to release the past?

17. Did I take appropriate breaks today? Do I have plans for a short or extended vacation to occur over the next few months?

18. Did I admit a mistake rather than rationalizing my behavior?

19. Did I ask for what I wanted?

20. Did I avoid or limit contact with a stress-producing person?

21. Did I create a peaceful atmosphere at home, work, and in my car?

22. Did I release tension by deep breathing, singing, or other God-honoring techniques?

23. Did I laugh several times throughout the day?

24. Did I consciously slow the pace at which I walked or talked?

25. Did I encourage or check on someone within my support system?

26. Did I avoid using "stress-speak" or terms that indicate rushing?

27. Did I remember to thank God for a disappointment He allowed?

28. Did I guard against self-sabotaging behavior that threatened my peace?

29. Did I emotionally relinquish a situation that was outside of my sphere of influence?

30. Did I maintain a positive outlook when faced with a negative situation?

Appendix B

Worry-Busting Scriptures

*Give all your worries and cares to God, for
he cares about what happens to you.*

1 Peter 5:7

*Be anxious for nothing, but in everything by prayer
and supplication, with thanksgiving, let your
requests be made known to God; and the peace of
God, which surpasses all understanding, will guard
your hearts and minds through Christ Jesus.*

Philippians 4:6-7 nkjv

*The Lord gives his people strength. The
Lord blesses them with peace.*

Psalm 29:11

*Cast thy burden upon the Lord, and he shall sustain
thee: he shall never suffer the righteous to be moved.*

Psalm 55:22 kjv

But blessed are those who trust in the LORD and have made the LORD their hope and confidence. They are like trees planted along a riverbank, with roots that reach deep into the water. Such trees are not bothered by the heat or worried by long months of drought. Their leaves stay green, and they go right on producing delicious fruit.

JEREMIAH 17:7-8

You will keep in perfect peace all who trust in you, whose thoughts are fixed on you!

ISAIAH 26:3

Come to me, all you who are weary and burdened, and I will give you rest. Take my yoke upon you and learn from me, for I am gentle and humble in heart, and you will find rest for your souls. For my yoke is easy and my burden is light.

MATTHEW 11:28-30 NIV

Peace I leave with you, my peace I give unto you: not as the world giveth, give I unto you. Let not your heart be troubled, neither let it be afraid.

JOHN 14:27 KJV

Yes, you will lie down and your sleep will be sweet.

PROVERBS 3:24 NKJV

About the Author

Deborah Smith Pegues is an international speaker, award-winning author, a Bible teacher, certified public accountant, and certified behavioral consultant specializing in understanding personality temperaments. Her books include the bestseller *30 Days to Taming Your Tongue* (over 850,000 copies sold), *Emergency Prayers*, and *Choose Your Attitude, Change Your Life*. She and her husband, Darnell, have been married for more than 35 years and live in California.

For speaking engagements, please contact her at:

The Pegues Group
P.O. Box 56382
Los Angeles, CA 90056
(323) 293-5861
Email: deborah@confrontingissues.com
www.confrontingissues.com